RECIPE DISCLAIMER

To the best of my knowledge, the recipes contained herein are original to me, though many were inspired by the remarkable chefs whom I've had the pleasure of working with over the years.

Published by Advantage, Charleston, South Carolina.
Member of Advantage Media Group.

ADVANTAGE is a registered trademark and the Advantage colophon is a
trademark of Advantage Media Group, Inc.

Printed in the United States of America.

First Printing, 2016.

ISBN: 978-1-59932-752-5
LCCN: 2016953058

Book design by George Stevens. Photography by Bob Waggoner.

The S.N.O.B.

SLIGHTLY NORTH OF BROAD

EXPERIENCE

FRANK LEE

Dedicated to
Malcolm Hudson, the Innoculator.

CONTENTS

Bill Hall

Owner, Hall Management Group

 Welcome to our family restaurant which we are extremely proud of: Slightly North of Broad, or as the locals say, "SNOB."

It was several years ago when we were fortunate enough to have our first experience of dining at S.N.O.B., due to our longtime dear friend Judge "Sol" Blatt, Jr. introducing us to the culinary king of Charleston, Chef Frank Lee's masterpiece. Judge told us this was the place to be. As soon as you walk in the door you see the powers of Charleston enjoying themselves. It felt as comfortable as if you were in your own home. One thing I noticed right away was the southern hospitality and genuine feeling of the staff, especially general manager Peter Pierce.

We never would have thought eight years ago that we would own this special piece of Charleston dining. We enjoy every day and each experience with old and new friends walking in the door.

This book is a view into the heart of Slightly North of Broad, and we hope you will enjoy each page as if you were sitting at the chef's table watching Frank Lee in action.

PHILOSOPHY OF THE
S.N.O.B. KITCHEN

W

HEN THERE'S ALL SORT of madness going on outside, the kitchen is the only place that makes sense.

You can't have chaos in a kitchen. Everything relies on a perfect balance, a sustained rhythm, that keeps plates swirling from station to station, spinning in concentric circles of *mise en place* that allow a dish to move from blank canvas to finished plate in fifteen minutes. In the rhythm of *mise en place*—everything in its place—each level supports the other. Things can branch off from one item to another, one station to another, picking up a little dab of reduced stock here, some minced shallot there, the recipes for the day describing the algebraic paths of hundreds of dishes through the kitchen microcosm.

Balance, too, is necessary in the kitchen, in your menu, and in your plates—and it has to reflect your personal life. You can't be an out-of-control maniac and expect to maintain balance in the kitchen. You have to have balance in your life to be able to take a life, treat it with respect, and transmogrify it in the cooking process with a positive energy so that it will nourish somebody and make him or her feel good. But it takes learning these rhythms, having balance, and understanding your responsibilities to achieve that.

Responsibility. You don't hear people talk about it, but it's as much a part of the kitchen as rhythm and balance. You're responsible for taking life. What we call freshness is simply the moment that is closest to death. You have to respect the ingredients you're using.

mise en place

every thing iN place

It's easy to think about this in terms of an animal, but think about a squash. First, someone had to prep the soil, then plant the seeds, nurture the seedlings, weed around them—cultivate them as they grew through the vagaries of the weather. Then they had to pick the squash at the right time, handle it correctly, get it to market, and sell it to you.

And you bring it home only to let it rot in the refrigerator? Come on. You've taken that life force. You are responsible for that process.

These three elements—rhythm, balance, responsibility—are the backbone of my philosophy on cooking. I didn't learn any of them quickly or easily. I bounced from place to place for ten years, learning technique from some amazing chefs and wrenching out something you might call style.

But I didn't start with that intention. In fact, I never planned on becoming a chef at all.

THE MILITANT VEGETARIAN

I got started in this crazy business by opening up a militant hippie vegetarian restaurant in Columbia, South Carolina, of all places, right out of high school in 1973, when I was seventeen years old.

I opened the restaurant, 221 Pickens Street, as a lark with three other friends, thinking we'd do it for the summer and then go back to college. We opened for a song and a dime and we built everything in that place, from the booths to the fans to the dry-food storage bins for bulk items like brown rice, oats, soy beans, you name it.

We advocated food for health, even though we were vilified for telling people that sugar, refined flour, and meat were bad for them. We were told we were un-American, but we stuck to it, despite the fact that we didn't know a thing about cooking when we opened the place. Hell, we literally didn't know how to boil water. Our first meal was pinto beans, boiled cabbage, sautéed squash, and brown rice.

We were fortunate to be located close to the state farmers' market, which was one of the main reasons our restaurant quickly evolved into a natural food co-op. It was also where I got a quick crash course in local and industrial food chains.

I soon learned the rhythm of when the farmers brought in the best stuff—usually around 4:00 a.m. on Monday—and I learned to appreciate their products. I began to understand the national and international companies that brought bananas from Guatemala, potatoes from Montana, and vegetables from all over.

I didn't have an agenda, I wasn't selling our restaurant as locally sourced and seasonal; it was what it was and what was available, so that's what we used.

That early time at 221 Pickens Street was what set me on the path of food for health that was fresh, seasonal, and local. But after about six years of that, I was getting restless.

What did intrigue me was French cuisine. That's when French rebels like Frédy Girardet, Michel Guérard, Paul Bocuse, and Roger Vergé were

young and bucking the system in France. I wanted to do what they were doing, and I was lucky to find someone who was doing real, honest-to-God French cooking in Columbia: Malcolm Hudson.

Hudson and I got along well. He had no formal training and was entirely self-taught. In the 1980s, when "French cooking" was considered opening a Knorr Swiss package to make hollandaise, whipping up a steak Diane, and serving *escargot* out of a can, Hudson was a lone wolf, who shunned *faux*-French for the real deal.

Barely a year into working with him, he took me on a trip to France with his *maître d'*. For three weeks, we traveled through France in a camper van, eating at nine three-Michelin-star restaurants in the dead of January.

Frank Lee, age 17.

It was a mind-expanding experience. I had never seen anything like what they were doing. I'd never even heard of it. These guys were artisan businessmen: masters of their craft, masters of business, operating at a level that was like going to the Louvre. It was a nexus, a conscious-altering moment that was inspirational.

The chefs we met were kind and generous. Every one of them invited us into their kitchens and every time

I expected to see some ingenious machination that helped them create masterpieces like the ones I'd eaten. But it was all blank tables and knives, stoves and refrigerators. Nothing that would tell you how they could create amazing artistry.

Up until that trip to France, I kept thinking that one day I'd go back to school to become a doctor lawyer Indian chief, the way I was raised. But seeing what they did in those French kitchens, I knew that my path was set. Here was something worthy. I was going to be a chef.

Before we left France, I remember asking Chef Paul Bocuse what advice he might have for a young American cook.

He smiled, looked me in the eye, and said, "Learn your technique. Apply it to your region. Don't copy us."

I didn't think much about it then, but those words have come back to me in spades over the years. It's what we've been trying to do at Slightly North of Broad since the day we opened: put those pieces together.

WRENCHING OUT A STYLE

The thing is, you can learn technique. You can learn your rhythm of *mise en place*, and you can become a good technician. It

When you have your techniques and you're applying them to your region, sourcing locally and paying attention to seasonality, you're creating a rhythm.

takes something more to get style. Style comes from your character, from your being. You have to find that and wrench it out of yourself. Just because you've conquered a technique doesn't mean you have something to say.

Take music. You learn to play scales, chords, arpeggios. You learn inversions and you get to the point where you can play folk songs, maybe some standards.

Then you might expand your repertoire and play the classics. Maybe you're one in a million and you become a virtuoso, playing Rachmaninoff on the keyboard. You're incredibly brilliant, but that doesn't make you a culinary composer, like Mike Lata of F.I.G. It makes you an incredible virtuoso technician.

But you can't find your style, your voice, until you have technique. Creativity doesn't come out of chaos; it comes out of control, repetition. That took me a while to figure out.

Today, when people come up to me and say, "I want to be a chef because I'm a really creative person," it depresses the hell out of me. It's like telling Picasso that you want to start painting like him because you're creative.

I tell them, "You want to be creative? Learn how to run the dish station on a Saturday night!"

Take barbecue, for instance. There are some great pit masters out there, like Rodney Scott and Sam Jones, who spent decades sweating over an open fire before they found their voices—and finding style with your technique is rare.

As Southern as Pad Thai

Over the years, we've developed some style at Slightly North of Broad. People want to put a label on us, that we're Southern, but it was never my intention to be a local-yokel restaurant or to be a Southern restaurant. I wanted to do French technique, apply it to the region, and try to wrench something out of myself that reflected who I am. The only label I've been okay with is "eclectic," and that's because that's what we are.

I mean, think about it. Were we a Southern restaurant? When we started, we had grilled pizza. We made our own pasta and served it three different ways. We had blinis with ossetra caviar. We had ribeye, filet mignon, pad Thai, and sesame tuna with nori rolls right along with butterbeans, quail, and okra stew.

That's what we're trying to do at S.N.O.B.: real cooking that has value, that's healthy, that's respectful and true to its nature, and that is available to the average Joe fifty, sixty times a year because it's at a price he can afford.

Julienne
Radish

LEARN YOUR TECHNIQUE—
APPLY IT TO YOUR REGION

Those themes—learn your technique and apply it to your region—are how we at S.N.O.B. approach our mission of bringing real food to real people. It means making our own desserts, sourcing locally as much as we can, and paying attention to the seasons. It means sharing our excitement about cooking and encouraging others to surpass us. It's about passing on the torch.

None of us made this stuff up, we didn't make up *paté au choux* or *crème brûlée*. It's all been passed on to us, done by the chefs before us and so on. We have to honor that and stay true to the technique and what they've created.

Certainly you can expand on it, but you have to pass on your knowledge about technique and how you learned your repertoire. You need to be able to teach people how to have hands, how to have a tongue, how to have a palette, how to cook—how to live.

When you have your techniques and you're applying them to your region, sourcing locally and paying attention to seasonality, you're creating a rhythm.

When a kitchen works well, it's because it has rhythm and balance. It makes sense.

RECIPES

I didn't learn how to cook from recipes but from guidance, practice, and repetition.

There are all sorts of nuances that you can't express in a recipe; they need to be learned. In a recipe for a *nappe* sauce, for example, the instructions can't accurately convey what it means when the sauce *shines*, when it's right to take it off the heat.

These things must be learned. No one gets good at something by merely doing it eight hours a day or by doing it whenever they feel like it. If you want to excel at something, you have to do it over and over again. One of my mentors, Yannick Cam, told me something that I still share with my cooks, "If you do something well fifty times, you haven't done anything. If you do a dish five hundred times correctly, you still haven't done anything. If you do it five thousand times, correctly and with no variation, then you've accomplished something."

No one wants to hear that. Most people want to be able to do something quickly, but we don't become good at anything overnight. It takes a minimum of ten or twenty years to become good at something. Mozart comes along every now and then, but not that often. It takes ten years of hard work and severe dedication to get truly accomplished at something, and that applies whether you're a doctor, lawyer, chef, writer, or any other profession.

Cook. Taste what you cook. Keep doing it, and don't get discouraged. Every mistake is a lesson learned, and even the simplest recipes can get screwed up if you're not paying attention. The result is commensurate to the amount of effort you put in. That training is integral to our kitchen. We eat, drink, dream cuisine.

CUISINE COMMANDOS

It's not uncommon, when new cooks join us at S.N.O.B., that they get inoculated with the spirit of cuisine, and within a year, somehow shed most of their previous accoutrements of life.

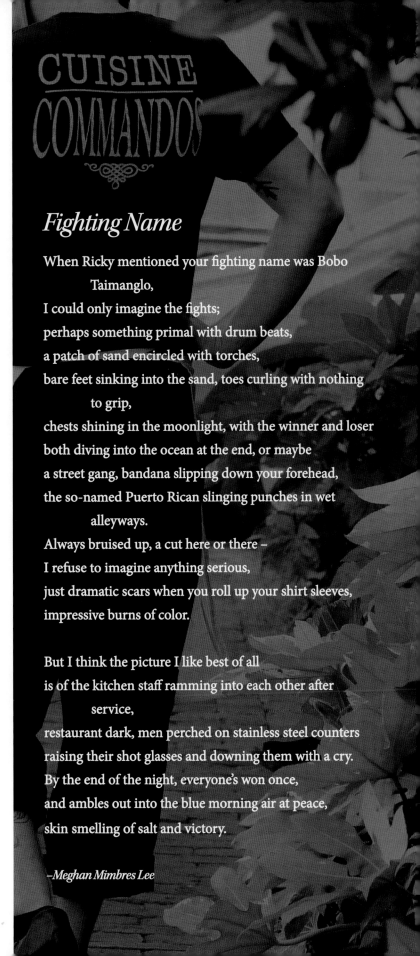

CUISINE COMMANDOS

Fighting Name

When Ricky mentioned your fighting name was Bobo
        Taimanglo,
I could only imagine the fights;
perhaps something primal with drum beats,
a patch of sand encircled with torches,
bare feet sinking into the sand, toes curling with nothing
        to grip,
chests shining in the moonlight, with the winner and loser
both diving into the ocean at the end, or maybe
a street gang, bandana slipping down your forehead,
the so-named Puerto Rican slinging punches in wet
        alleyways.
Always bruised up, a cut here or there –
I refuse to imagine anything serious,
just dramatic scars when you roll up your shirt sleeves,
impressive burns of color.

But I think the picture I like best of all
is of the kitchen staff ramming into each other after
        service,
restaurant dark, men perched on stainless steel counters
raising their shot glasses and downing them with a cry.
By the end of the night, everyone's won once,
and ambles out into the blue morning air at peace,
skin smelling of salt and victory.

–Meghan Mimbres Lee

They are now in the kitchen crucible, where impurities are burned off and they're focused solely on the rhythm and balance of the kitchen and the cuisine. They have walked through fire, and their dedication is as evident as the burns of battle on their hands and arms. They go into combat every day having each other's backs, willing to sacrifice and willing to dedicate themselves to the chef and the cuisine.

For those few, I came up with the term *Cuisine Commando.*

The Cuisine Commando shirts are given out sparingly. You have to work years to get one. It's a blood shirt. It means that you have been, and will be, valiant under fire and dependable in combat, and that you believe in what you do.

Those who have earned these shirts have them still. They're dear and special to them, and having one gives them a sense of belonging.

We don't have a name for the network of cooks, chefs, food-and-beverage lifers that exists in Charleston, but it's a beautiful thing. We don't disparage one another. If someone has an idea and another chef finds a new way to run with it, we cheer them on, we encourage them, because that's part of passing the torch.

A Cuisine Commando also has a unique opportunity in the S.N.O.B. kitchen. It's one of the ways we create our daily menus and it's why you'll never see the same thing twice on our specials: you're given the opportunity to create.

At S.N.O.B., you may come in, proudly wearing your Commando shirt, and I may immediately say to you, "You've got triggerfish. You need to use up sweet potatoes. We've got zucchini, and there's a bunch of leeks and shishito peppers. You have thirty minutes. Tell me what you want to do."

Of course, I already have an idea of what I want to do. I can't say, "Fix whatever you want." You have to look at the entire picture—not only the dish but how it plays holistically into the rhythm and balance of the kitchen.

That's what a lot of the specials at S.N.O.B. are. They're the result of our *sous-chefs* coming up with an item that works within these constructs, that takes into account our responsibility, uses our technique, and applies it to our region. Our daily sheet is how we express that ephemeral, seasonal creativity, and it's where you find a lot of the personality at Slightly North of Broad.

YOUR CHALLENGE

That's also why writing a cookbook for Slightly North of Broad was a challenge. We use recipes—but we also use methods and techniques. We've had our classics, those sacred cows that over time had to be chopped from the menu, not because they weren't popular but because they were *overly* popular. They'd become such a part of our repertoire that they were keeping us from staying relevant in the culinary scene.

Where our personality is, where we stand out, is in our dailies, those *a la minute* menu items that evolve from what we have available from our farmers: several pounds of this or that produce, a few dozen cuts of various protein, and the *mise en place* already set at our stations.

Here you'll find our staid and popular dishes and our long-running seasonal plates that can be found on our menu three, four, maybe even five months

out of the year. But the dailies are *your* challenge. This book will give you the preparations for several of our more widely used sauces and stocks, garni and side dishes. I'll share with you how to prepare the focal point, be it fish, beef, or veggie. But it's on you to bring them together, to use what you have around you and to use up what ingredients you have, to show respect to the lives you've taken and to create balance within the rhythm of your own kitchen.

Because the kitchen is not simply a room: it is a study, it is a workshop, and it is an altar. It is where we go to lay bare the essence of life and transmogrify it in a way that makes it delightful and nourishing. It is a place of balance and rhythm, integrity and quality, responsibility and joy.

COCKTAILS

THE FIRST THING YOU'RE asked when you sit down for lunch or dinner at S.N.O.B.—or any restaurant—is "What can we get you to drink?" Each of these drinks has a story, and every bartender at S.N.O.B. knows them. In fact, the best part about S.N.O.B. cocktails is our bartenders. The repertoire they've had over the years with clients is incredible—for customers, the drinks they're enjoying are always complemented by the great hospitality they receive.

Wine is IMPORT

Patrick Emerson
Owner of Curated Selections

Wine and food pairing should be a fun, not stressful, experience. It's good to remember that "most wines go with most food most of the time." Once you learn the basic structures of different wines, pairing is more of an art than a science. The only way to really see if that fabulous Pinot gris from Alsace is going to be perfect with the S.N.O.B. pad Thai dish is to try it out. Chef Lee and I spent many joyous hours writing wine dinner menus together, and we had a lot of great hits. Sometimes however, the pairing that worked best on paper, and that we felt sure was going to inspire, fell flat. My humble advice is to concentrate more on matching the wine with the weight of the dish (light, medium, heavy), and focus on the sauce rather than the main protein. Don't chase the flavors of the dish; rather, let the wine coax them in. Complement the flavors—don't imitate them—and have fun experimenting!

It balances out aggressive flavors, lends characters to subtleness, and adds dimensions in *ways that only wine can.*

IF YOU'RE SMART ENOUGH and lucky enough, every now and then you pair the right wine with the right food so that the individual tastes transcend each other into an almost indescribably sublime experience. It's a goose-bumpy sensation that doesn't happen very often, but when it does, it's dramatic.

I was fortunate enough to have the torch of wine knowledge passed to me early on in my career—from Jovan Trboyevic with his fabulous cellar, where he enlightened me to many of his wines, to Yannick Cam, who probably had one of the best burgundy cellars in the nation. Hudson was the same way. They all wanted us to know what fine wine was, so

we drank just about every vintage and varietal of wine you could name. At no point did any of them say, "This bottle cost $200," or something like that. Instead, they'd pull a dusty bottle off the shelf and say, "Try this, you'll like this one."

Wine is important. It balances out aggressive flavors, lends character to subtleness, and adds dimensions in ways that only wine can. At the same time, though, there's no given. Just because you have a great cabernet and a great chunk of beef, or a great burgundy with pigeon and foie gras and truffles, that doesn't mean they're going to hit it off. They may complement each other very nicely, give a nice handshake, but they don't necessarily come together in that orgasm that can transcend all conscious thought.

Sometimes it's difficult for sommeliers to know what to serve with some of the dishes we have at S.N.O.B. What do you serve with barbecued tuna? What do you serve with asparagus and egg salad with lemon zest? What do you serve with kimchi? But Patrick Emerson, owner of Curated Selections who worked with us as a sommelier for eight years, did a great job of it. We collaborated on many, many dinners, and he always came up with excellent pairings. I owe a lot of my wine education to his knowledge and fine taste.

Christmas Eve Eggnog

This is one of those things that's been taken down to its lowest common denominator, so when people have fresh eggnog with freshly grated nutmeg, they're blown away. It's a far cry from that terrible, guar gum-thickened, artificially flavored substance you find in the store around Christmas. But you make it fresh, and it's like a fluffy, drunken crème anglaise with nutmeg.

We only serve this at Christmas Eve lunch, along with sugar cookies. It's a drink that will change your attitude, and it's not for lightweights.

Tools needed: 2-gallon pot, bowl of ice, microplane

Yield: 1 gallon

Ingredients:

12 eggs, separated	2 cups bourbon
1 pound powdered sugar	1 cup brandy
4 cups milk	
4 cups cream	1 cup rum
1 teaspoon vanilla	1 fresh nutmeg

Method:

- Beat the egg yolks and sugar in pot, then mix in the milk.
- Cook over medium heat, whipping constantly until the custard begins to thicken, then quickly place the pot in the bowl of ice.
- Continue to beat mixture until it's cool, then add cream and liquor.
- Whip egg whites to soft peaks and gently fold into eggnog.
- Garnish with fresh grated nutmeg to taste.

The Barnraiser

YIELD

1 drink

TOOLS NEEDED

rocks glass

THIS IS ANOTHER COCK-TAIL that's close to my heart. We created it not long after Annie Filion of Keegan-Filion Farm lost her barn in a fire. We had a big fundraiser scheduled for her to help her rebuild, but the event was months away. In the meantime, we made cocktails, donating one dollar from each drink sold to help Annie rebuild her barn, and raised about $5,000.

After the event was over, we tried to take it off the menu, but the bartender refused. "People love this drink, don't take it off," she said.

"Well," I said, "if it's going to stay, it needs a name."

Someone said, "Call it the Barnraiser."

The name stuck, and it's still on the menu today.

Ingredients

2 oz. bourbon
¼ oz. dark honey
2 dashes orange bitters
2 oz. Blenheim's Spicy Ginger Ale
orange peel for garnish

Method

Mix bourbon with honey.

Add bitters and ginger ale.

Pour over ice and garnish
with orange twist.

Jamaican Bobsled

YIELD

1 drink

TOOLS NEEDED

muddler, tall glass

T HIS ISN'T SOME-THING THAT would be served on the S.N.O.B. menu, few at that time shared my love of old Jamaican Rhum, but it would be served to me. It's basically a mojito with rum, mint, lime, ginger ale, and a splash of club soda, and it's been my lifesaver at the end of a long day. After twelve or thirteen hours straight, I like to wind down by working in the dish room, which is relaxing to me. But it's even more relaxing if I can get a Bobsled.

Ingredients

2+ oz. Jamaican rum, dark

1 oz. Blenheim's Spicy Ginger Ale

2+ oz. seltzer

¼ of a fresh lime

2 sprigs fresh spearmint

Method

Muddle 1 sprig spearmint with the rum.

Squeeze the lime juice in and toss in the fruit, too.

Add the seltzer and ginger ale.

Pour over ice and garnish with remaining mint sprig.

The Iceberg

THIS IS NOT A drink for light-weights. It sounds like a simple drink, but the fun is to shake it until the ice cracks into tiny pieces. When served, there has to be a top of tiny, crunchy icebergs. So far, I've only met two bartenders in Charleston who can perform this drink, Trevor at S.N.O.B. being one of them.

"The result is commensurate with the effort."

Ingredients

7 oz. vodka

½ oz. limoncello

ice

Method

Fill shaker to the top with ice, add liquor, and shake until hand freezes to shaker or arm goes numb. Strain into rocks glass, releasing the icebergs.

Peach Sangria

Tools needed: wine glass

Yield: 4-6 servings

Ingredients:

2 freestone peaches: ripe, firm, halved, and sliced ¼"thick

½ fresh orange, cut into fourths

½ fresh lemon, cut into fourths

2 oz. pineapple juice

1 liter *Pinot Grigio*

1 oz. brandy

1 oz. peach schnapps

1 oz. triple sec

seltzer or club soda

lemon-lime soda

Method:

- Mix all but the seltzer and lemon-lime soda together and macerate, refrigerated, overnight.
- To serve: put 5 oz. sangria with pieces of the fruit in a large wine glass, add ice, a splash of seltzer, and lemon-lime soda.

Variation

Replace peach with fresh strawberries or pears

Charleston Cocktail

Served on the rocks, enjoy!

Tools needed: tall glass

Yield: 1 serving

Ingredients:

2 oz. Firefly Sweet Tea Vodka

splash of unsweet tea

¼ oz. mint simple syrup

2 oz. fresh-squeezed lemonade

SOUPS

ONE OF THE THINGS that has set S.N.O.B. apart for so many years is our selection of soups. It's a branch of making stocks, a vehicle for seasonality, and a way we can show respect for using things up and making things taste good. It's all my wife ever wants when we go out—soup and a salad. But it's harder and harder to find it. Maybe I'm a dinosaur, but I love soup, and we serve an enormous amount of it every week.

Red Bean Soup

YIELD

12-14 servings

TOOLS NEEDED

2-gallon pot with lid

URING THE EARLY 1980S, I spent a fair amount of time visiting friends in NOLA and taking in its many regional dishes. This recipe is a tip of the hat to a quintessential New Orleans dish—red beans and rice, inspired by Buster Holmes. Our version is vegetarian, though you can always add your own andouille or **Kielbasa Sausage** (*p. 69*).

Ingredients

1 pound dry red beans

1 tablespoon garlic, medium-diced

1 cup carrots, medium-diced

2 cups onion, medium-diced

1 cup celery, medium-diced

2 cups bell pepper, medium-diced

1 jalapeño, seeded and medium-diced

½ cup olive oil

2 tablespoons salt

~2 quarts water

2 tablespoons chili powder

2 tablespoons cumin powder

6 tablespoons paprika

2 tablespoons chipotle in adobo sauce

Method

Cover the dry red beans with water and refrigerate overnight.

The next day, sweat down all vegetables with salt and garlic until soft.

Add dry spices and continue to cook for another 2 minutes.

Drain the beans, rinse, and add to mix along with water and chipotle.

Cover pot and simmer for 3 hours until beans are very tender.

Purée half of the soup in a blender and mix back in with the whole beans.

To serve, top with Tomato **Jalapeño Cilantro Salsa** (*p. 167*) and sour cream.

Cream of Green

YIELD	TOOLS NEEDED
6–8 servings	2-gallon pot, blender, fine *chinoise*

CREAM OF GREEN IS a great example of responsibility, using up green stems that so often get thrown away. Made well, this is an intensely flavored, silky canvas on which to project other textures like sautéed mushrooms, roasted fennel, or diced celery. Have respect—use it all up.

Ingredients

3 oz. bacon, small-diced

2 cups yellow onion, small-diced

2 cups celery, small-diced

2 teaspoons salt

1 oz. butter

6 cups tender green asparagus stems, sliced thin

2 cups potatoes, peeled and small-diced

1 quart chicken stock or water

½ cup parsley, medium-diced

1 cup heavy cream

Method

In a large pot, sweat the bacon down, rendering the fat without browning it.

Add the butter, onions, celery, and salt, and cook until soft.

Add the asparagus and cook, covered, over medium heat, stirring often until the asparagus turns bright green and gives up its juice.

Add the potatoes and chicken stock and simmer, covered, until the potatoes are soft.

Add cream and purée in blender with parsley until parsley is liquefied, enhancing the green color.

Pass through a fine *chinoise* before serving.

VARIATION

Omit the parsley and feature a white vegetable, such as celery root, kohlrabi, or turnip.

Not grooving on the bacon? Leave it out!

Gazpacho

YIELD	TOOLS NEEDED
6–9 servings	nonreactive bowl

WHEN THE TEMPERATURE IN Charleston hits 90 degrees or more—which is most of our summer—we put gazpacho on the regular menu. This recipe is one my dad worked out years ago, and it reflects two things: the rhythm of the seasons and knife skills. When you're making enough for lunch and possibly dinner at S.N.O.B., you have to dice up an enormous amount of vegetables by hand, to the point where you might get carpal tunnel syndrome after a few years.

Ingredients

½ cup red wine vinegar

2 teaspoons salt

¼ teaspoon garlic, minced

½ cup red onions, small-diced

1 cup green bell pepper, small-diced

1 cup celery, small-diced

1 cup cucumber, seeded, small-diced

2 cups yellow tomato, peeled, seeded, medium-diced

2 cups red tomato, peeled, seeded, medium-diced

1 cup watermelon, seeded, medium-diced

2 cups water or watermelon juice

2 cups Sacramento™ tomato juice

2 tablespoons olive oil

2 teaspoons mint leaves, medium-diced

Method

Macerate onions, garlic, and salt in the vinegar as you dice the other vegetables

Add vegetables (hard to soft) as you cut them; the vinegar and salt will soften them up.

Add tomato juice and watermelon juice (or water) and refrigerate for at least one hour.

Use olive oil and diced mint to garnish each bowl.

Oyster Stew

This is our attempt at a classic, simple South Carolina oyster stew. It's adapted from one of the dishes Yannick Cam made at le Pavillion in D.C., although he would make it into a custard with jumbo lump crab and garnish it with belon oysters.

This stew has huge flavors, with smoked bacon, scallop cream, oysters that are barely cooked, potatoes, and leeks. It's a classic, but it also reflects our quality and integrity, and it works with our rhythm of service.

Tools needed: 2 skillets

Yield: 4 servings

Ingredients:

1 cup Yukon gold potatoes, peeled and medium-diced

1 cup white of leek, sliced thin

1 tablespoon butter

½ cup apple smoked bacon, medium-diced

1 cup **Scallop Cream** (*p. 141*)

24 shucked oysters

pinch salt

~1 cup water

1 tablespoon minced chives

Method:

Sweat leeks with butter and salt in a skillet until tender, ~2 minutes.

Add the potatoes and cook for ~5 minutes or until tender, without browning and moistening with water as needed.

Dice bacon and cook in skillet until the fat has rendered and bacon is a light brown. Drain.

Add scallop cream to potato/leek mixture and warm together over medium heat.

When hot, stir in the oysters and bacon, barely cooking the oysters (they're done when they've crinkled around the edges), and hit it with the chives and a pinch of freshly ground black pepper before serving.

Okra Gumbo
with Neck Bone, Pig Tail, and Ham Hock

YIELD	TOOLS NEEDED
12-14 servings	2-gallon pot

ANOTHER SUMMER SOUP THAT stays with us most of the way through fall is okra gumbo. We make the soup in a stock made from smoked neck bone, pig tail, and ham hock, which we got for the longest time from Marvin's Meats in Hollywood, South Carolina. Big G, one of our longtime cooks at S.N.O.B., taught me how to cook those down real slow in a big pot of water, strain it off, and pick the meat off the hocks, tails, and neck while it was still hot. The result is an incredibly silky, rich, well-balanced, flavorful, basic okra gumbo that can be a standalone or enhanced as you choose.

Ingredients

2 cups onion, medium-diced

2 cups bell pepper, medium-diced

1 cup carrot, medium-diced

4 cups tomato, peeled and medium-diced

4 tablespoons olive oil

1 teaspoon salt

½ teaspoon pepper

1 teaspoon sugar

8 cups **Neck Bone, Pig Tail, and Ham Hock Stock** (p. 172), defatted

1 pound meat from neck bone stock, medium-diced

1 teaspoon Tabasco

1 tablespoon fresh thyme, medium-diced

2 fresh bay leaves

2 pounds okra, sliced ½" thick

Method

*When the Vegetable Bin on East Bay was in business, I could spend 30 minutes in competition with home cooks picking through the okra to obtain the smallest, most tender **Okra** (p. 76). At S.N.O.B., we thicken our gumbo with okra, not roux. Gumbo, okra ... to me, it's the same word.*

In a large pot, sweat the vegetables with the olive oil, salt, and pepper.

When soft, add the tomatoes and diced meat from the stock, and cook for 5 minutes over medium heat.

Add the stock, thyme, bay leaves, sugar, and Tabasco.

Bring to a simmer, then add the okra and let simmer another 5 minutes.

Pam Zaresk

S.N.O.B. is quite simply my home—where my heart is. And like any good home, it's been my nurturing place, from the excellent food to the staff that warms my heart with each and every encounter. The S.N.O.B. "experience" has drawn me back regularly (sometimes three or four times a week) since I first came to Charleston in 2002. S.N.O.B. is the soul of Charleston, and it is, quite simply, the best.

Thai Curry Butternut Squash

YIELD	TOOLS NEEDED
8-10 servings	2-gallon pot, blender, *chinoise*, food processor (optional)

IN THE LATE FALL, we start running our butternut squash soup with a red Thai curry paste, which imparts those great seasonings of lemongrass and ginger, and add in coconut milk, finishing the presentation with a garnish of toasted pumpkin seeds.

Butternut squash is a classic winter vegetable and one that we often pair with other winter crops, such as fennel, celery root, and turnips.

Ingredients

4 cups butternut squash, peeled, seeded, medium-diced

2 cups carrots, peeled, medium-diced

1 cup onion, peeled, medium-diced

2 cups apple, peeled, cored, medium-diced

1½ tablespoons red Thai curry paste

1 tablespoon salt

½ cup olive oil

3, 12-oz. cans coconut milk

4 tablespoons honey

1 cup toasted pumpkin seeds

½ cup sugar in the raw

1 quart water

Method

Sweat butternut, carrot, onion, apple, red Thai curry paste, salt, and olive oil, in the pot, stirring often, until the squash is well cooked, falling apart, and giving up its juice. If the mixture starts to stick, add water as needed to moisten.

Add coconut milk and enough water so that the mixture is covered and cook over low heat until the vegetables are soft.

Add honey, then purée mixture in blender and pass through a *chinoise*.

Pulse toasted seeds with sugar in a food processor or chop finely by hand and use the seed mixture as a topping.

Beef and Black Bean Chili

YIELD

12-14 servings

TOOLS NEEDED

2-quart pot, 2-gallon pot

WE ORIGINALLY MADE THIS chili for one of the first SPCA Chili Cook-Offs hosted by Kay Hyman in the early 2000s. Bob Waggoner, Robert Carter, and I were often judges, and local celebrities—including fire chief Rusty Thomas, and radio personalities T.J. Phillips and Tanya Brown—would compete every year. They'd trash talk each others' chili and get more elaborate in their presentations, to the point where one year the fire department delivered their chili to the rooftop restaurant where the competition was being held using a ladder truck—sirens wailing and firemen in full gear running up the ladder to drop it off.

But there was never enough chili, so we started making our own, about five gallons or so, to take with us.

It was never our intention to make chili for any other reason than the SPCA Cook-Off, but one cold winter day we decided to put it on the specials menu.

Ingredients

1 pound ground beef

2 cups onion, medium-diced

2 cups bell pepper, medium-diced

2 cups carrot, medium-diced

1 tablespoon salt

1 tablespoon pepper

2 tablespoons chili powder

3 tablespoons cumin powder

3 tablespoons smoked paprika

2 tablespoons garlic, medium-diced

4 cups tomato, peeled and medium-diced

6 cups water

2 cups dried black beans

2 tablespoons chipotle in adobo, medium-diced

Method

Add enough water to the black beans to cover them, and then leave them to soak overnight in the refrigerator.

The next day, drain and simmer in a 2-quart pot with water for 2 hours until very tender. Set aside.

In a 2-gallon pot, brown the ground beef over high heat, then strain off most of the fat; add the onions, bell pepper, carrots, and salt.

Cook until the vegetables are soft, then add spices and garlic, cooking for ~5 minutes to activate the spices without burning them.

Add the tomatoes and black beans along with their liquid and the chipotle. Turn heat down and simmer for 30 minutes.

Serve with corn chips.

Cream of Crab Soup

YIELD	TOOLS NEEDED
4-6 servings	2-gallon pot, whisk

OUR VERSION OF THE she-crab soup is a roux-thickened seafood bisque with a bit of diced carrot to give it the orange roe color, since female crabs are off-limits in the southeast.

The final touch—a good serving of high-quality aged Madeira—speaks to Charleston's colonial roots (even though this soup, a nineteenth-century invention, does not), and the bisque and Madeira certainly enjoy each other's company.

Ingredients

¼ pound butter

2 cups onion, fine-diced

1 cup celery, fine-diced

½ cup carrot, fine-diced

1 teaspoon salt

½ teaspoon white pepper, ground

1 bay leaf

¼ cup flour

1 quart **Shrimp or Fish Stock** (*p. 172*)

½ cup cream

½ pound crab meat

¼ teaspoon mace, ground

2 shakes Tabasco

½ cup high-quality sherry or Madeira

Method

Melt the butter in the pot and add the onion, celery, carrot, salt, and bay leaf. Cook until soft.

Add the flour to make a roux with the vegetables, cooking ~ 5 minutes and stirring continuously.

Add the hot stock and whisk until soup boils, then reduce to simmer.

Simmer 5 minutes, then add cream, mace, and white pepper. Simmer another 5 minutes.

Add crab right before serving, finishing with the oldest, finest-quality Madeira you can find.

Blue Crab Consommé with Corn and Leeks

I learned this soup from Yannick Cam at le Pavillion in D.C. You want to use the freshest, clearest stock for a bright, clean taste.

Tools needed: 2–quart pot, whisk

Yield: 4 servings

Ingredients:

2 tablespoons butter

2 cups white and light green of leek, cut into thin semi-circles

¼ teaspoon salt

1 cup **Cooked Fresh Corn** (*p. 78*)

1 pound jumbo lump crab

1 quart **Chicken Stock** (*p. 171*)

6 garlic cloves, peeled and lightly scored

1 teaspoon fresh thyme buds

pepper

Method:

- Melt the leeks in the pot with butter and salt. Don't let them brown!
- Add cooked corn and chicken stock and bring to a simmer.
- Add the garlic.
- Add crab, thyme, and pepper to taste, keeping crab lumps as intact as possible.
- Remove garlic after one minute.

SALADS

LIKE OUR SOUPS, WE have some salads that never leave the menu, others that might run for three months, and some that reflect our creativity and spontaneity—that use up whatever's coming in the front door, fall into our rhythm of *mise en place*, and dance on the palate.

Grilled Salmon Salad

YIELD	TOOLS NEEDED
1 serving	grill or skillet, bowl

Ingredients

6 oz. salmon filet, skinless

salt

pepper

2 oz. spinach, cleaned

3 grape tomatoes, halved

1 tablespoon **Pickled Banana Peppers** (*p. 180*)

1½ oz. Split Creek Farm feta goat cheese

½ navel orange, supreme (segments without pith, membrane, or seed)

½ oz. radicchio, sliced thinly

~1 oz. of **Lemon Shallot Dressing** (*p. 177*)

½ avocado, sliced

Method

Season the salmon filet with salt and pepper to taste.

We like to grill our salmon, but pan searing is also fine. A 6 oz. filet, paillard, or cut on a slight bias, will cook up mid-rare in ~3 minutes.

Toss the spinach, tomatoes, pickled banana peppers, goat cheese, oranges, and radicchio in a bowl with the vinaigrette.

Mound the salad high and place the salmon on top, finishing with the slices of avocado.

WE'VE HAD SALMON ON our menu since day one. Some people take umbrage with the fact that it's neither local, seasonal, nor Southern—but it's a fish our customers like and a lot of the customers who like it are locals.

We've had a salmon salad in different variations over the years, but this is the one that stuck. It's healthy, beautiful, light, and perfect for lunch.

Terri Henning

S.N.O.B. is home to me. It's family, it's great food, and it's comfort. Comfort in knowing that Peter will greet me with a big smile and laughter. Comfort in knowing that after fifteen years, Frank still comes out to catch up and say thank you for joining him and the family for a meal. The grilled salmon salad is my go-to.

Fried Chicken Watermelon Salad

YIELD

1 serving

TOOLS NEEDED

cast iron skillet, bowl, deep-fry thermometer (optional)

I ORIGINALLY PUT THIS ON the menu as a lark, thinking it would be fun to say "fried chicken" and "watermelon" in the same sentence. I had no idea it would be so popular, but people love it. We only run it for two months out of the year, while the watermelons are at their peak.

Ingredients

6 oz. chicken breast, cut into 4 long strips

1 cup buttermilk

1 batch **Calabash Crumbs** (*p. 123*)

1 cup canola oil

4 large cubes of watermelon, cut 1" square

2 oz. goat cheese

2 tablespoons **Candied Pecans** (*p. 43*)

3 grape tomatoes, cut in half

1 oz. **Red Wine Dijon Vinaigrette** (*p. 176*)

2 oz. arugula

Method

Marinate chicken breast in buttermilk overnight.

Heat oil until temperature is 325°–350°.

Toss chicken strips in calabash crumbs, then fry in oil until cooked and golden brown (~ 6–8 min.). Drain strips on newspaper and keep hot.

Toss arugula, crumbled goat cheese, watermelon cubes, and candied pecans (see next page) in a bowl with the red wine Dijon dressing.

Lay the hot chicken strips on a serving plate and mound the salad on top.

Candied Pecans

Tools needed: 2-quart pot

Yield: 2 cups

Ingredients:

2 cups pecans, halved

1 cup sugar

½ cup water

½ teaspoon salt

¼ teaspoon cinnamon

⅛ teaspoon cayenne

Method:

- Pre-mix the salt, cinnamon, and cayenne.
- Combine the sugar and water in the pot and bring to softball stage (235°).
- Add the salt/spice mix and nuts and stir vigorously, coating nuts evenly.
- Remove from heat and pour nuts onto a baking sheet to cool.

Grilled Peach Salad

YIELD

2 servings

TOOLS NEEDED

grill or grill pan

THIS SALAD IS A reflection of the seasonal rhythm of the peach. We wait until late June, early July, to serve because that's when the freestone peaches grown in South Carolina are ripe. We'll dip the halves in a little sugar, grill them so that they get nice marks, and serve them with very thin slices of prosciutto or Allan Benton's country ham with a salad made with toasted nuts and Split Creek Farms goat cheese.

Ingredients

1 whole freestone peach, cut in half

2 oz. prosciutto or country ham, sliced very thin

4 oz. mixed greens

2 oz. goat cheese

1 oz. **Balsamic Vinaigrette** (*p. 176*)

1 pinch coarse salt

Method

Choosing a ripe, firm peach is critical. Halve the peach by cutting it from stem to bottom, opposite the natural seam and through the circumference of the peach. Give the peach a gentle twist so that, when the halves are separated, the seed is poking out rather than lying flat and, thus, easily removed.

Dip the cut side of the peach in sugar and grill cut-side down long enough to create marks and heat the peach.

Lay the thinly sliced ham on the plate, top with the dressed greens, place the warm peach on top, and finish with a quenelle of local goat cheese.

-cut opposite the natural seam

Peach pit stands up

Celeste Albers

Green Grocer

The word that best describes S.N.O.B. is hospitality: sincere, nurturing hospitality. Everyone at S.N.O.B. is part of a team, truly a family, and they open their arms to embrace you and bring you into that family.

S.N.O.B. was one of the first restaurants to buy product from us. Chef Lee took a genuine interest in our farm and also in our family. His enthusiasm for fresh, quality produce and his lively, caring nature are inspirational. My daughter, Erin, grew up accompanying me on restaurant deliveries; three times per week we went through S.N.O.B.'s back door. The special attention she received there had a profound influence on her.

Chef Lee was a fresh local-food pioneer. Long before there was a "buy local" and sustainable seafood initiative, he was buying from local purveyors. More importantly, he looked for ways to help them to build a sustainable business. I don't believe Green Grocer would be in business today were it not for the love and support of Chef Frank Lee and S.N.O.B.."

Caramelized Pear Salad

YIELD	TOOLS NEEDED
2 servings	propane torch, 2-quart pot

FOR AS LONG AS I can remember, I've been on a quest to make people eat pears. We've tried pear almond tartlet, poaching pears in red wine or port and served with vanilla syrup and ice cream, or vanilla-poached pear with tarragon ice cream, which was fabulous—couldn't give it away.

Finally, one of the S.N.O.B. cooks came up with this salad. It has an almost ephemeral nature to it, with the slightly warm pear, crunchy *brûlée*, and tart cheese. It also has a trick to it, in that the poaching liquid needs to be reduced down to a syrup and then poured over the pear, which then needs to be sugared and *brûléed* quickly or else the caramelization won't stick.

I didn't think this dish had a chance in hell, but it sells like crazy. We serve it from late fall through early spring, about five months out of the year.

Ingredients

1 Bosc pear, peeled, halved, and cored
1 quart **Pear Poaching Liquid** (*P. 47*)
2 oz. mixed greens
1 oz. blue cheese
1 oz. pistachio nuts, shelled and toasted
1 oz. dried cranberries
1 oz. **Honey Key Lime Dressing** (*P. 177*)
1 oz. honey
1 oz. sugar

Method

Follow pear poaching liquid directions on next page.

Remove chilled pears and pat dry.

Drizzle the pear halves with honey or syrup and dust with sugar. Immediately *brûlée* with torch and serve each pear half over mixed greens tossed in dressing.

Pear Poaching Liquid

I thought the citric acid in a lemon kept things from browning. Wrong—it's the ascorbic acid in vitamin C. Who knew? Karen Barker, owner and pastry chef of Magnolia Grille in Durham, NC, did...

Ingredients:

2 cups water

1 cup sugar

1 tablet vitamin C

1 lemon, cut in half

1 star anise

Method:

· Boil ingredients until sugar dissolves, then reduce heat and add prepared pears.

· Cover with parchment paper and cook gently 10–12 minutes until tender.

· Cool completely and store in syrup, if needed.

Charleston Crab Salad

YIELD

4 servings

WE SELL THIS SALAD all year long at lunch and consider it a real reflection of our region. It's your grandmother's crab salad, with crab claw meat bound with mayonnaise, lemon, basil, bell pepper, and shallot. We serve it with fresh fruit, a little salad, and a hardboiled egg.

Ingredients

1 pound crab claw meat, picked
2 tablespoons shallots, fine-diced
2 tablespoons bell pepper, fine-diced
2 tablespoons fresh lemon juice
½ teaspoon salt
½ teaspoon pepper
4 tablespoons mayonnaise
2 tablespoons fresh basil, medium-diced

Method

Mix all ingredients together and serve.

Sautéed Chicken and Arugula Salad

This is a standard that we run about six or seven months out of the year, usually from late fall to early spring. We use local products as the seasons allow, with apples from North Carolina and arugula from local farms like Pete Ambrose's on Johns Island.

Yield: 1 serving

Tools needed: skillet

Ingredients:

6 oz. chicken breast, cut into 8 pieces

salt

pepper

1 oz. country ham, sliced into strips

1 tablespoon olive oil

2 oz. arugula

½ Granny Smith apple, peeled, cored, and sliced thinly

2 tablespoons pecan halves, toasted

2 tablespoons blue cheese

1 oz. **Balsamic Vinaigrette** (*p. 176*)

1 tablespoon dried cranberries

Method:

- Heat olive oil in skillet.
- Season the chicken pieces with salt and pepper to taste and place in hot skillet, allowing the pieces to brown by not stirring them around.
- When browned, flip the pieces over and add the country ham, cooking until the chicken is done.
- Toss all ingredients in a bowl so that the hot chicken and ham slightly wilts the arugula and cheese.

Replace chicken with **Duck Confit** (*P. 145*)

Bryan Austin

head server,
Charleston Grille

I spent three years at S.N.O.B.: 2002–2005. I started as a server's assistant with no front-of-house experience, but they took a chance on me.

I attribute so much of what I do and why I do it to Chef Lee. His passion for food, his reverence for the farmers, his love of the staff that look at him as a father, and his understanding of the art of "the tableside" are all unparalleled.

Chef Lee taught me to describe food with "mouth-watering terms." Rather than "an arugula salad," he'd describe "a salad of arugula." He'd talk about the farm where it was grown and the families that grew it, even as those families brought fresh produce in the kitchen. I watched, on numerous occasions, Chef Lee reject invoices from Celeste Albers, saying, "You're not charging me enough, charge me more."

Chef Lee taught me the core, basic principles of what we, in the restaurant industry, should all be doing. We are here to serve. We are here to create dining experiences. We are here to bring joy to people's lives.

APPETIZERS

FROM DEVILED CRAB CAKES to shrimp mousse-stuffed squash blossoms and this tuna crudo (pictured), our appetizers are a reflection of fresh ingredients done in a classic manner.

Shiitake Mushroom
Filled with Foie Gras Mousse

YIELD	TOOLS NEEDED
4 servings	2, 10-inch skillets, 2-gallon pot or wok

WE STARTED FEATURING FOIE gras back in the ''90s when not a lot of people were doing it, especially in the South, and we wanted to make sure it was something our customers could afford to try.

This recipe uses a **Foie Gras Mouss**e (*p. 67*) that I learned to make from Yannick Cam in DC, which is half chicken and half foie gras. For the mushrooms, we originally used shiitake from Ben Cramer on Johns Island, and today we get them from Mepkin Abbey out in Monck's Corner. It's a great example of French technique applied to our region.

Ingredients

16 medium shiitake mushrooms, de-stemmed

1 pound **Foie Gras Mousse** (*p. 67*)

3 tablespoons butter

1 pound spinach, de-stemmed

2 oz. water

⅛ teaspoon salt

4 oz. **Port Wine Reduction Sauce** (*p. 175*)

Method

Preheat oven to 350°.

Fill the white side of the mushroom with 1 oz. mousse.

Heat 1 tablespoon butter each in both skillets and place the mushrooms cap-side down, cooking gently for 5 minutes.

Flip the caps and place in 350° oven for 5 minutes or until internal temperature reaches 150°.

In pot or wok, heat 1 tablespoon butter, salt, and water and quickly sauté the spinach 1–2 minutes.

Strain spinach and keep warm until ready to serve.

Mound spinach in a bowl and place 3 caps around and 1 on top. Sauce with 1 oz. port wine sauce.

Shrimp Mousse-Stuffed Squash Blossoms

YIELD	TOOLS NEEDED
4 servings	piping bag, skillet

SQUASH BLOSSOMS ARE A wonderful representation of French technique with local ingredients. In Charleston, farmer Pete Ambrose on Wadmalaw Island grows wonderful squash blossoms every year that still have the little fruit attached. Into this we'll pipe a shrimp mousse—a fabulous recipe that I pretty much stole from Bob Waggoner, of *In the Kitchen* with Chef Bob Waggoner. It's an ephemeral dish because you never know when you're going to get the blossoms, and it's dramatic in its presentation: the yellow blossom with the green or yellow fruit, the pink mousse, and the *coulis* or butter sauce. It's one of the dishes that I feel speaks of S.N.O.B. and its unique rhythm, technique, and style.

Method

Using a piping bag, fill 8 squash blossoms with 1–2 oz. **Shrimp Mousse** (p. 66) each.

Gently poach blossoms in water in a skillet, covered, until mousse is fully cooked, ~5 minutes.

Serve with **Shallot Butter Sauce** (p. 165) and Parisian scoops of blanched vegetables.

Parisian scoops

Stone Crab Cocktail

NOT MANY PEOPLE HARVEST stone crabs commercially, but for a while we were getting ours from Kimberly Carroll of Kimberly's Crabs out at Shem Creek in Mount Pleasant. She would bring us the most beautiful, fresh stone crab claws, and we'd carefully cook and shuck them so that the meat was still intact in this big claw, ready to go. We'd use the arm of that meat and make cocktails with orange segments, chunks of avocado, micro-greens from City Roots up in Columbia, and grape tomatoes from one of our local producers, like Holy City or Kurios Farms. It's a beautiful dish that features fresh, local ingredients in a classic manner.

Ingredients

4 pounds cooked stone crab claws

1 shallot, minced

3 tablespoons orange juice

juice of 1 lemon

4 tablespoons olive oil

salt

pepper

12 cherry tomatoes, halved

orange segments from 2 navel oranges

6 large leaves basil (green or purple), cut into fine ribbons

Method

Shell the stone crab, keeping the claw's shape intact.

Make a dressing by mixing together minced shallot, orange and lemon juices, olive oil, salt, and pepper.

Lightly toss the crab, orange segments, and tomatoes with the dressing. Serve in cocktail glasses, finishing with fine ribbons of basil.

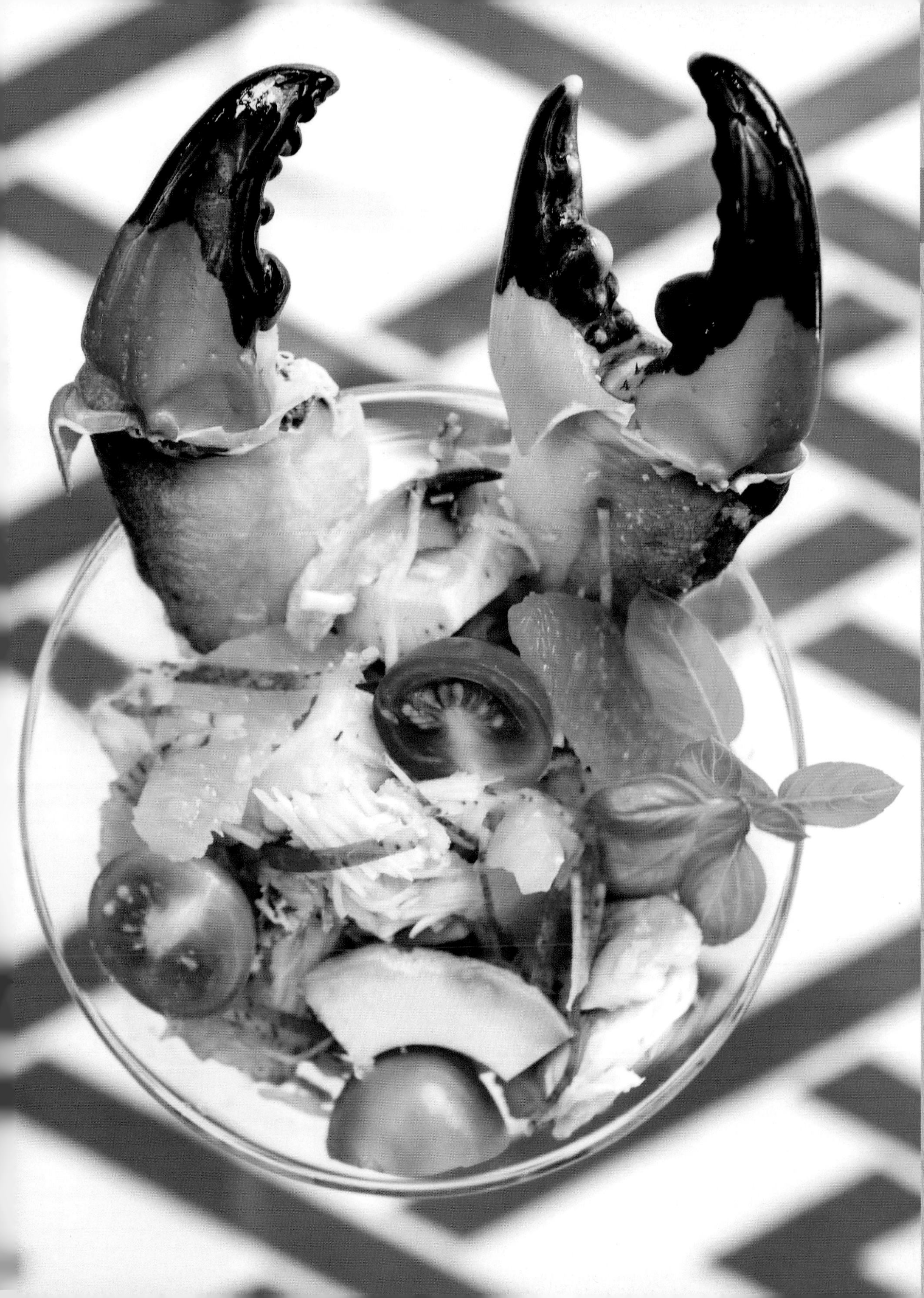

Tuna Crudo

KEN VEDRINSKI INSPIRED ME with his stunning crudos. In turn, I ripped off his delightful garnishes and applied them to tuna. This dish has become one of our go-to dishes for dinner parties and other off-premise events because it's so dramatic, and if it's your first course, you're golden—everyone's hungry!

It uses the tender heart of the tuna, sliced thinly and garnished with wonderful ingredients like pickled jalapeños, garlic, orange segments, radishes, micro-greens, crispy little potato chips, avocado, olive oil, and sea salt. It's a visually stunning party in the mouth, and it's easy to make.

Method

Place 2 oz. thinly sliced eye of tuna loin on a plate and drizzle with olive oil and salt.

Strew with sliced avocado, **Pickled Garlic and Jalapeño** (p. 181), and some pickling juice.

Add 1 orange supreme (segments without pith, membrane, or seed), julienned radishes, and micro-greens in Haiku fashion; finish with potato chips.

House-Smoked Salmon

WHEN I WAS GROWING up in Chicago, my dad would take me to the Berghoff for smoked salmon, and it was always an intensely flavored, melt-in-your-mouth, wonderful treat for me.

At S.N.O.B. we learned how to make it ourselves, packing it in a mixture of equal parts salt and sugar, holding in refrigerator for three days, then washing it off, drying it out, and **Cold Smoking** it in a homemade smoker that anyone can make at home (see next page). When it's done, it can be used in any one of dozens of applications. A handful of the ones we've featured over the years are:

- Wrap around fried oysters and serve with a smear of blended goat and cream cheese topped with a little vinaigrette and cucumbers.

- Put on hot rye toast with cream cheese and pickled onions.

- Chop and mix with capers and goat cheese, and use it to fill a paté a choux.

- Serve with a tart salad and caper vinaigrette.

Smoked Salmon Cure

YIELD
4 cups

TOOLS NEEDED
9 x 13 pan,
plastic wrap

Ingredients

1, 5-pound side of salmon, skin on and belly trimmed

2 cups salt

2 cups sugar

1 teaspoon Instacure #1 (or 1 teaspoon per 5 pounds meat)

Method

Mix salt, sugar, and Instacure well.

Put salmon in pan, pack with mixture, cover with wrap, and refrigerate for 3 days.

Cold Smoking

After curing, you can cold smoke just about any protein using a 6-inch-deep steam table pan, two bricks, and a screen. I think the bricks we have at S.N.O.B. have been used for about twenty years, and they're completely black now.

All you need to do is build a fire of wood chips in the pan and then smother it. Then put the bricks in the pan with the screen across the top of them, place your protein on the screen, cover it with foil, and let it sit in the refrigerator overnight. With our smoked salmon, we let it percolate in those fumes for about 12–24 hours until we have a nice, very acceptable smoked salmon.

You can cold smoke just about anything: vegetables, pork chops, cheese ... whatever you think would taste good smoked.

CHARCUTERIE

THE CHARCUTERIE AT S.N.O.B. started out of necessity and exemplifies our rhythm of *mise en place* when it comes to butchering pigs and duck and rabbit. When you have a local pig come in with a fat cap of about four inches, you have to do something with the fat, the head, and the meat between the ribs. It isn't the price; it's a matter of having respect for the animal and staying in the rhythm and balance of our *mise en place*.

It's the French technique applied to our region, and over the years we've tried to make it our own. We were the first in town to start doing it in the early 1990s. Craig Deihl, over at Cypress, is doing a marvelous job with his cured meats, which is exciting because in the end, it's about passing the torch—and we're proud to cheer him on. That's the kind of camaraderie we have in Charleston.

Country Pâté

Rillette

Liver
Mousse

Sausage

Pork Rillettes

YIELD	TOOLS NEEDED
2-4 servings	2-quart pot with lid, 2, 4 oz. ramekins

RILLETTES ARE BASICALLY A cold French barbecue, with lots of fat and herbs and mustards packed into it. It's the original cold, potted meat, and we mainly make it from duck, pork, or rabbit, depending on what we have in and what we need to use up.

Ingredients

PART I

1-pound pork butt, cut into 3" cubes

½ leek, bottom portion

1 celery rib

½ yellow onion with root intact

5 cups **Chicken Stock** (*p. 171*)

1 teaspoon black peppercorns, whole

6 sprigs thyme

4 cloves, whole

3 garlic cloves, smashed

PART II

1 tablespoon whole grain mustard

1 tablespoon Dijon mustard

1 tablespoon salt

2 teaspoons pepper

1 tablespoon sherry vinegar

1 cup rendered pork fat

1 teaspoon thyme, picked

Method

Put all Part I ingredients in pot, cover, and bring to a very light simmer. Cook for ~ 2½ hours or until fork-tender.

Pull the pork out of the cooking liquid and discard vegetables.

Pull the meat with a fork and mix in the Part II ingredients and half the pork fat.

Divide the pork into 2, 4-oz. ramekins and seal with the rest of the pork fat. Chill.

Variation

For a **Rabbit Rillette***, use rabbit meat instead of pork butt, and replace mustard and sherry vinegar with tarragon, parsley, and lemon juice.*

Duck Liver Paté

YIELD	TOOLS NEEDED
2-4 servings	food processor or blender, *tamis* (optional), two 4. oz ramekins

FOR THE PATÉ, WE cook down the livers from the whole ducks with brandy, Madeira, thyme, and bay leaf, purée it all up, and add in soft butter, finishing it off with a touch of cream and more booze. Then we pass it through a *tamis* (drum sieve) to get the consistency super smooth. Then we put it in a mold and top it off with a little duck fat or pork fat to seal it from the air.

Ingredients

1 pound duck livers, connective tissue removed, rinsed, and patted dry

½ cup shallots, peeled and sliced

3 tablespoons butter, room temperature

¼ teaspoon Instacure #1

¼ cup fine Madeira, plus 1 tablespoon to finish

¼ cup brandy

1 sprig fresh thyme

1 bay leaf

1 teaspoon salt

½ teaspoon white pepper

¼ teaspoon paprika

2 tablespoons crème fraiche

2 tablespoons rendered duck fat, pork fat, or butter

Method

Remove connective tissues from livers, rinse, and pat dry.

Sautee cleaned livers with 1 tablespoon butter, ½ teaspoon salt, white pepper, bay leaf, thyme sprig, and Instacure #1 until just cooked through.

Let cool for 10 minutes, then discard thyme and bay leaf. Set cooked livers aside.

In the same pan, sweat the shallots with 1 tablespoon butter and ½ teaspoon salt until tender. Add the brandy and Madeira and reduce by two-thirds.

Put the livers, boozy shallots, and paprika in a food processor or blender and purée until smooth.

Add the last tablespoon butter and finish with the crème fraiche and 1 tablespoon fine Madeira.

Optionally, pass mixture through a *tamis* for additional smoothness and consistency.

Place mixture in ramekins and seal with rendered fat or butter.

Christina M. Couture

Cuisine Commando 1993–2003; general manager, Cypress Restaurant

I started working at S.N.O.B. a few weeks after it opened, and it was evident at the beginning what a special place it is. Chef Frank Lee was our leader, our teacher, our friend. He inspires loyalty that is truly rare these days and used sustainable, local food before it was hip or cool simply because it was the right and honorable thing to do. He patiently answered questions and usually gave you a great story to go along with it. I became an adult at S.N.O.B.; I grew up here, I love it here.

Country Paté à la S.N.O.B.

YIELD

12-14 servings

TOOLS NEEDED

spice grinder (coffee grinder); meat grinder with 1/4" meat grinder plate, chilled; electric mixing bowl with paddle attachment; 13³/⁴" x 4¹/²" le Creuset paté terrine with lid; deep pan big enough to hold terrine

BETWEEN DISCOURSES ON NIETZSCHE, Beethoven, and sensimilla, Malcolm Hudson taught me how to make this classic country paté.

Ingredients

3½ pounds pork butt, cubed medium

3 tablespoons salt

2 teaspoons pistachio oil

¾ teaspoon Instacure #1

1 cup yellow onion, fine-diced

2 tablespoons thyme, medium-diced

2 teaspoons pepper

1 cup port wine

1 cup dried cranberries

1 tablespoon olive oil

2 tablespoons **Paté Spice Blend** (recipe below)

¼ cup cold water

1 cup shelled pistachios

12 slices (¾ pound) thin-sliced bacon

6 fresh bay leaves

6 sprigs thyme

PATÉ SPICE BLEND

1 tablespoon whole allspice

1 tablespoon whole clove

1 tablespoon whole coriander

1 tablespoon nutmeg, freshly grated

½ teaspoon cayenne, ground

½ teaspoon cinnamon, ground

Method

Preheat oven to 300°.

Place ¼"grinder plate for meat grinder and bowl for electric mixer in the refrigerator to chill.

Cube pork butt and chill.

Lightly toast pistachios in a 350° oven for 2–3 minutes or until fragrant.

Toast paté spice blend in a sauté pan over low heat until fragrant, then grind all in a spice grinder (or very clean coffee grinder).

Dice and sweat onion in olive oil until soft, then add dried cranberries and port and reduce by ⅔. Place boozy mix in refrigerator to cool completely.

Remove grinder plate and cubed pork from refrigerator and grind the pork through meat grinder once. Chill pork and grinder plate for 15–20 minutes, then grind pork a second time.

Mix 2 tablespoons paté spice blend with salt, pepper, thyme, pistachio oil, Instacure #1 and cold water.

Put ground pork, spice/water mixture, onion/cranberry mixture, and toasted pistachios in chilled electric mixer bowl with paddle attachment and mix at low speed 1 minute.

Line terrine mold with thin-sliced bacon.

Add *paté* mixture and fold hanging bacon over top.

Top bacon with bay leaves and thyme sprigs.

Place lid on top of terrine and lightly tap mold on table to pack down mixture.

Place terrine in pan and pour hot water into pan until it comes halfway up the sides of the terrine.

Bake at 300° for 90 minutes or until the internal temperature reaches 150°.

VARIATION

Add 6 oz. chilled puréed liver, duck, chicken, or pork to meat mixture; raise finished cooking temperature to 160°.

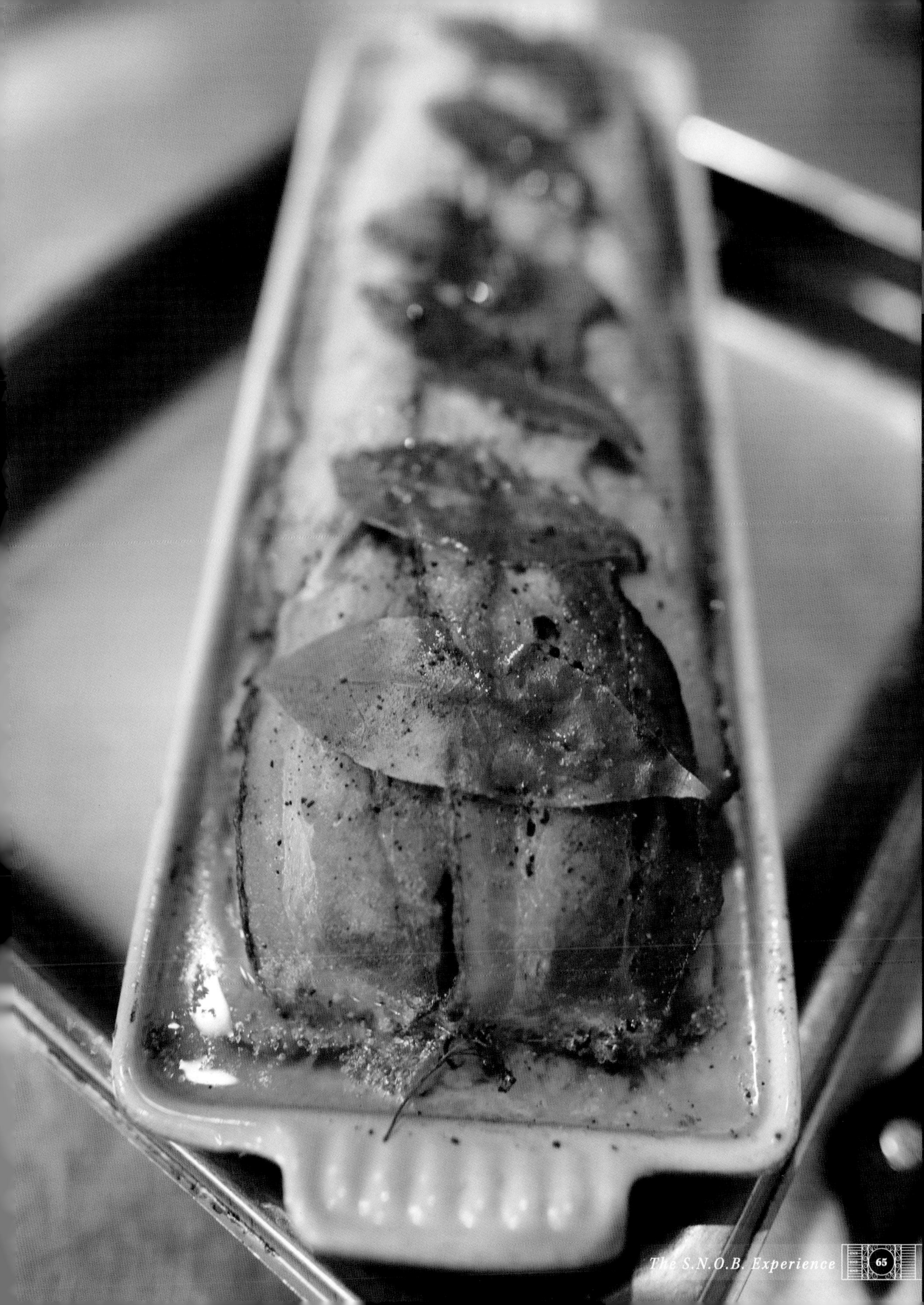

MOUSSES

T HE TRICK TO ANY mousse is to make sure you keep everything cold, so put the basket and blade of your food processor in the freezer about 15 minutes before making any of these recipes.

Shrimp Mousse

Tools needed: food processor, stainless steel bowl, bowl of ice

Yield: ~3 cups

Ingredients:

10 oz. shrimp, peeled and deveined

1½ teaspoons salt

1 pinch white pepper, ground

½ cup shallots, fine-diced

1 tablespoon chives, fine-diced

1 tablespoon tarragon, fine-diced

1½ cups cream, cold

Method:

- Put cleaned shrimp in a stainless steel bowl, placed on top of a bowl of ice.

- Purée shrimp, salt, and pepper in chilled food processor.

- Put shrimp purée back in chilled bowl and let it relax for ~15 minutes.

- By hand, beat in ½ cup of cream at a time.

- Mix in herbs and shallots.

- Keep cold until ready to serve.

OTHER USES

Shrimp mousse, and in fact all of the mousses we make, are one of the many ways we use things up and show respect for the creature. There are dozens of ways it can be used, such as:

- Make little "sausages" by spreading mousse on buttered tin foil, adding a baton of quick-seared zucchini seasoned with madras curry, rolling up the tin foil ends to form a small shrimp sausage and cooking quickly.

- Use the mousse to make small tarts.

- Make a flounder *paupiette* by lightly pounding the flounder filet and smearing the inside with shrimp mousse. Lay down fresh julienned vegetables so that the ends are just poking out over the edge, roll it up, and bake.

- Pipe the mousse in little dollops into hot water, like gnocchi, then chill and use to garnish sautés or cream soups.

Chicken Mousse (For Stuffing)

This is a denser, more neutral mousse that compliments chicken and **Quail** *(p. 112)* and won't squeeze out of the stuffed item while cooking. Omit the tarragon, and the mild mousse takes on the flavor of the host. We also use this to fill the rabbit loin and belly for the **Rabbit Roulade** *(p. 155)*.

Tools needed: food processor, stainless steel bowl, bowl of ice

Yield: about 2 cups

Ingredients:

12 oz. boneless, skinless chicken breast, fine-diced

1 teaspoon salt

¼ teaspoon white pepper, ground

½ cup cream, cold

1 tablespoon fresh tarragon, medium-diced

1 tablespoon chives, minced

2 tablespoons shallots, minced

Method:

- Put diced chicken in the stainless steel bowl and place on top of ice bowl. Refrigerate 10–20 minutes.

- Purée chicken in chilled food processor for 3–4 minutes.

- Transfer purée back to chilled bowl and refrigerate another 10 minutes.

- Beat in chilled cream by hand, adding pepper, tarragon, shallots, and chives at the end.

- Keep cold until ready to use.

Foie Gras Mousse

Tools needed: food processor, stainless steel bowl, bowl of ice

Yield: about 2 cups

Ingredients:

6 oz. chicken breast, small-diced

4 oz. foie gras grade "A", small-diced

1 teaspoon salt

1 cup cream

¼ teaspoon white pepper, ground

1 tablespoon fresh truffle, fine-diced (optional)

2 tablespoons shiitake mushrooms, fine-diced, cooked in butter and chilled (optional)

Method:

- Place diced foie gras, chicken breast, and salt in stainless steel bowl over bowl of ice and refrigerate 15 minutes. Chill food processor bowl and blade.

- Purée foie gras/chicken mixture in chilled food processor in half increments, returning puréed mix to ice bowl and refrigerating another 15 minutes.

- Beat in cold cream ⅓ cup at a time, beating significantly until the mousse shines.

- Keep cold until ready to serve.

Grouper Terrine

YIELD

12–14 servings

TOOLS NEEDED

13³/⁴" x 4¹/²" le Creuset paté terrine with lid, food processor, stainless steel bowl, bowl of ice, deep pan to hold terrine mold, meat thermometer

Ingredients

20 oz. grouper, small-diced

2 teaspoons salt

4 egg whites

2 cups cream

2 tablespoons chives

2 tablespoons tarragon

1 cup shallots, fine-diced

½ teaspoon white pepper, ground

1 cup snow peas, blanched and julienned

1 cup carrots, blanched and julienned

Method

Heat oven to 350°.

Sprinkle salt over diced grouper and place in a stainless steel bowl; set over bowl of ice to keep cool.

Pulse grouper in chilled food processor in two batches until you have a very smooth paste. Chill.

When both batches are done, return the full amount of fish paste to the processor and pulse in egg whites.

Return mix to chilled bowl and chill for 10 minutes.

By hand, beat in cream in three batches.

Add herbs, shallots, snow peas, and carrots.

Line terrine mold with plastic wrap, fill with mousse, cover, and place in deep pan, partly filled with hot water.

Place in oven and bake at 350° for 40 minutes, or until the internal temperature of the mousse reaches 150°.

Serve with **Leek Cream** (*p. 126*) or **White Wine Cream Sauce** (*p. 163*).

House-Made Kielbasa Sausage

YIELD

2 pounds

TOOLS NEEDED

meat grinder with 1/4" grinder plate, electric mixing bowl with paddle attachment, sausage press and natural hog casings to make link sausage (optional)

I N THE EARLY DAYS of S.N.O.B. we purchased sausage, but as we got in pork shoulders and butts with our loin, we started to make our own simple kielbasa. These days, we probably make three 20-pound batches a week. It's an enormous amount of work but a great way to use up what we have.

Ingredients

2 pounds pork butt, cut into 2" cubes

2 teaspoons salt

½ teaspoon sugar

1 teaspoon garlic cloves, minced

1 tablespoon pepper, coarse ground

1 teaspoon fresh marjoram, medium-diced

½ teaspoon Instacure #1

3 tablespoons cold water

Method

Refrigerate grinder plate, electric mixer bowl, and cubed pork butt at least 15 minutes before making.

Grind chilled pork through chilled meat grinder once. Chill pork and grinder plate for 15–20 minutes, then grind a second time. Once finished, chill thoroughly.

Finely chop garlic and marjoram, then mix with salt, sugar, Instacure, pepper, and water.

Mix in well-chilled mixing bowl with chilled paddle attachment for ~1 minute on low–medium speed.

OPTIONAL: use sausage press and natural hog casings to make link sausage.

Lemon Sausage for Quail

This is a surprising juxtaposition of flavors, with the rich pork, the bright lemon, and the complex sesame. The combination marries well with the quail.

Tools needed: meat grinder with ¼" grinder plate, electric mixing bowl with paddle attachment.

Yield: 1 pound (enough to stuff 6 quail)

Ingredients:

1 pound pork butt, cut into 2" cubes

½ teaspoon salt

¼ teaspoon pepper

1 tablespoon lemon zest

¼ teaspoon Instacure #1

1½ tablespoons benne seeds, toasted (optional)

1 tablespoon thyme, picked

2 tablespoons parsley, medium-diced

Method:

- Refrigerate grinder plate, electric mixer bowl, and cubed pork butt at least 30 minutes before making.

- Grind chilled pork through chilled meat grinder once. Chill pork and grinder plate for 15–20 minutes, then grind a second time. Once finished, chill thoroughly.

- Mix in well-chilled mixing bowl with chilled paddle attachment for ~1 minute on low–medium speed.

the
technique
and rhythm of
VEGETABLES

THESE ARE SEVERAL OF the techniques we use for preparing our rhythm of vegetables at S.N.O.B., from methods to Sunday supper sides. The types of vegetables and grains we use vary by season and availability, but the following are our heavy hitters, the ones you'll almost always find on the menu in one form or another.

Blanching vegetables.

HOW TO BLANCH GREEN VEGETABLES

This is carved in stone: blanch your green vegetables in salted water.

It doesn't matter if it's broccoli, green beans, brussels sprouts, or any other green vegetable, it needs to be cooked in water that is as salty as the ocean: about a cup of salt per gallon. Boil the salted water in a large pot with a lid on it so you can keep it boiling hot and add in small amounts of green vegetables as you go. Cook them until tender and then shock the vegetables by quickly dropping them into and out of an ice bath.

How long do you cook your green vegetables? Until they're done. This is one of those techniques that you need to learn and develop over time. They're done when they're tender. How do you know they're tender? Take a bite and test them. It's a valuable skill to develop and when you do it right, it's almost a miracle.

ROASTING VEGETABLES

We roast vegetables in different ways, depending on what we want to do with them. A lot of times we'll dice the vegetable up in a *brunoise* and then toss that in a little bit of olive oil, salt, and pepper. We'll lay that out on a sheet pan in a single layer and roast until everything's nice and hot and aromatic.

Other times we want to roast a vegetable to bring out its intense sugar—like sweet potatoes that have been washed, lightly oiled, and roasted in the skin until right before the sugar runs out of them and burns the pan.

You can do the same with all root vegetables, roasting them until they're super tender but haven't given up their sugars. Then, when they cool down, you can scoop them out and make incredible purées that can be a simple mash or incorporated into **Custards** (*p. 74*), pies, or soups, or used to enrich risotto.

Onion, fennel, turnip, yellow squash, mushrooms, and beets

How long do you cook
your green vegetables?

Until they're done.

This is one of those techniques that you

need to learn and develop over time.

can be greatly enhanced with roasting. The process intensifies the flavor, and what you do with it after that is a matter of preference.

PURÉE VEGETABLES

We love to play with different types of purée at S.N.O.B., taking a root vegetable like celery root, turnip, or parsnip and cooking it down in milk or cream with onions or shallot and a pinch of salt until it's super tender and most of the liquid has evaporated.

What you're left with is a super, intensely flavored purée that you can put in a blender, food processor, or even a food mill and mash up. You can take a smear of roasted beets, for example, a tiny little puddle of snow-white celery root purée,

and put a nice piece of fish on top of it with a little radish salad, some pea shoots, and some fresh herbs—and suddenly you look like a magician, even though it's all quite simple.

Celery Root Purée

Tools needed: 2-quart pot

Yield: 2+ cups

Ingredients:

4 cups celery root, cleaned and medium-diced

1 cup onion, medium-diced

1 bunch fresh thyme, bound with string

2 cups milk

2 bay leaves

½ teaspoon salt

Method:

Simmer all ingredients until milk has almost evaporated.

Remove bay leaves and thyme, and purée remaining in food processor.

Kevin Johnson

chef/owner, The Grocery

"I came into the S.N.O.B. kitchen at the perfect time in my career—when I knew absolutely nothing. Frank Lee instilled a perfect mix of love, food, discipline, determination, and the importance of developing people—not just cooks. Little did I know his kitchen was different. I spent less than two years there, but these ideals have remained with me throughout my career. His genuine interest in my development since I left has been humbling. Even though I have been fortunate enough to be considered Frank's peer, I will always regard him as my mentor."

VEGETABLE CUSTARDS (CASSEROLE)

I learned how to make the custards we serve today during my stint at Le Perroquet in Chicago with Jovan Trboyevic, where we would do them as little timbales of puréed vegetables as a centerpiece for a sauté of crawfish or shrimp or scallops or squab livers. They'd call it a "custard," and I guess they were: a kind of small puréed vegetable casserole.

So we built on that. If the French are doing custards and we love eating vegetable casserole, I reasoned that we could bridge those ideas and bring them to fruition on a plate within 15 minutes.

Yellow Squash Casserole

We also use this recipe for roast butternut squash purée, cauliflower purée, cooked broccoli, spinach, etc.

Tools needed: 6, 4-oz. ramekins, deep baking dish

Yield: 6, 4-oz. servings

Ingredients:

1¾ cups **Country-Style Yellow Squash** *(p. 91)*

2 eggs

2 egg yolks

¼ heaping cup goat cheese

1 cup cream

¼ teaspoon nutmeg, fresh grated

¼ teaspoon salt

¼ teaspoon white pepper, ground

Method:

· Butter baking vessels and preheat oven to 325°.

· Mix all ingredients until well combined, then pour equal amounts into ramekins.

· Place ramekins in baking dish and fill dish with hot water until halfway up the sides of the ramekins.

· Bake ~1 hour, allowing 10 minutes for custards to relax before unmolding.

· Custards should be wriggly, rich, and delicate. Be gentle.

ONION

People ask me all the time what three ingredients I couldn't live without, and I always tell them, "Onions, salt, and olive oil." Onions are one of those things I could never do without. We've had several dishes over the years that were basically caramelized onions, cooking them down and down and down until they're a dark golden brown.

Caramelized Onions

YIELD	TOOLS NEEDED
2 cups	2-gallon pot

WHEN CARAMELIZING ONIONS, YOU want to cook them to where the sugars are perfectly developed but not burnt. It takes 30–40 minutes to get them where you want them … and then the phone rings and in the 30 seconds you're gone, the whole thing is burnt.

When caramelizing onions, you've got to stay with it. But when you do, it can lead to so many other dishes.

Ingredients

8 cups Palmetto sweet yellow onions, sliced

4 tablespoons olive oil

½ teaspoon salt

Method

Cook the onions, salt, and olive oil in the pot over medium heat for 30–40 minutes, stirring frequently.

When the onions reach a golden caramel color, you're done.

From here, you can go a hundred directions, using the onions in a jus, in the **Madeira Sauce** [*p. 175*], as a base for French onion soup, in a caramelized onion tart, or as a sauce for fish (right).

Caramelized Onion Sauce for Fish

To the adjacent recipe, add:

Ingredients:

1 jalapeño, seeded and sliced

4 garlic cloves, sliced

¼ cup fresh lemon juice

¼ cup parsley, medium-diced

¼ cup cilantro, medium-diced

Method:

- Add the jalapeño and garlic to golden sweet onions.

- Continue to caramelize without burning for 10 minutes.

- Add the lemon juice and herbs just before serving.

OKRA

I love okra six ways from Sunday, but I'm particular about it. It's one thing if you're using them in stews, gumbos, or soups. In those cases, you want to use the bigger okra, cutting them in nice, thick slices, checking for tenderness beforehand by pushing on the very top so that it snaps. If it doesn't snap, the okra will be fibrous and inedible. But the best okra for eating on its own, *al dente*, are the delicate small ones.

A lot of people say they don't like okra because it's too slimy, and it is when you cook the crap out of it. But when you've got tender okra and you can blanch it hot and al dente and crispy, it's wonderful and sublime, with a great texture and bite to it.

Method

For me, the best use for small, whole okra is in a little sauté, barely getting them hot in the pan with a little butter and salt and hitting them with enough water to steam them bright green and al dente, using them to garnish fish or meat.

TOMATOES

Tomatoes are another vegetable that we do every which way you can think of. We make marinara, we make **Tomato Coulis** [*p. 168*], we make salsas, we peel them, smoke them, roast them—it goes on and on.

peel your tomatoes!

When tomatoes are the star of a dish, you want to peel them. That's something I got from my mom and it's one of the things I'm adamant about.

Method

To blanch and peel a tomato, you have to core it and score it, blanching it quickly in boiling water (you don't need salt for this one) and placing it briefly in an ice bath. Don't let it sit any longer than it needs to in the ice bath—fifteen seconds can do it. Otherwise it gets waterlogged.

If done correctly, a properly blanched tomato is a thing of beauty. The flesh is not pulpy, it's glistening, firm, nubile; it looks wonderful.

The end result of your work is commensurate to the amount of effort you put into it. It doesn't matter if you're peeling a tomato, boning out a leg of lamb, sautéing a piece of fish, or shucking oysters. You have to try hard and do it exactly right. It's all part of the triumvirate of balance, rhythm, and responsibility.

Tomato Salad

Colors, sizes, and shapes are featured in a salad with frilly greens, cucumber, olive oil, reduced balsamic, and Bull's Bay Saltworks Red Mash sea salt.

CORN

There's a technique to taking corn off the cob. You can't cut it too deep, and you need to scrape out that sweet kernel juice after you've shaved off the corn. At S.N.O.B., we take all that and cook it down with a little diced onion and a little butter and sometimes chicken stock (though usually water) and cook it long enough so that it comes to a boil and cooks for a moment, getting it into stasis so that it doesn't spoil.

Cooked Fresh Corn

YIELD	TOOLS NEEDED
4 cups	skillet, baking sheet

COOKED CORN IS A seasonal color on the palate of our *mise en place*. We use it in the **Corn Butter Sauce** (right) that goes with our **Jumbo Lump Crab Cakes** (*p. 138*), it's a component in our succotash as well as some of our relishes and salsas, we sauté it with other vegetables ... the uses go on and on. Cooking corn like this holds the flavor for a few days, as fresh corn rapidly loses its sweetness as its sugar turns to starch.

Ingredients

4 ears sweet corn, cut off the cob and cob scraped (reserve juice)

1 cup sweet onion, small-diced

2 tablespoons butter

½ teaspoon salt

½ cup water

Method

Remove kernels from shucked corn with a shallow cut to avoid slicing into the tough cob.

Scrape the cob with the edge of your knife to harvest the remaining kernel and juice.

In a skillet, sweat the onion with butter and salt until tender, add the corn, and sauté quickly until hot, then add the water and steam until the water is almost evaporated.

Spread on a baking sheet and chill quickly.

Corn Butter Sauce

At the moment before service, we'll hit that cooked corn with a little bit of chicken stock—the lifeblood of our kitchen—and get it all bubbly and hot and just the right texture.

How much corn? How much chicken stock? It's hard to say; you have to work with it until it suits your tastes. We'll mount that with butter, making a sauce out of it, and garnishing it with fresh thyme.

Tools needed: skillet

Yield: 4–5 cups

Ingredients:

2 cups **Cooked Corn** (left)

4 oz. **Chicken Stock** (*p. 171*)

½ teaspoon salt

1 teaspoon fresh thyme, medium-diced

2 tablespoons butter

2 tablespoons shallots, minced

Method:

- Sweat shallots in a teaspoon of butter.

- Add the corn and chicken stock, bring to a boil, then turn down heat and stir in butter, thyme, and salt.

1000 dinners, Bob never had the same dish twice.

Grits

YIELD	TOOLS NEEDED
4 servings	pot with lid

PHILLIP BARDIN OF THE Old Post Office on Edisto Island put grits on the culinary map as much as anyone. Mine never tasted as good as his did—probably because I didn't have that Edisto water. We cook ours thicker than most, as we serve it with that saucy **Shrimp and Grits** (*p. 132*).

Ingredients

3½ cups water

½ teaspoon salt

2 tablespoons butter

1 cup stone-ground grits

¼ cup cream

Method

Bring water, salt, and 1 tablespoon butter to a boil.

Stir in grits.

Reduce heat to low and cook, covered, stirring occasionally, until grits are thick and creamy, ~40 minutes. Remove from heat and finish by stirring in cream and remaining butter. Keep warm until ready to serve.

Bob and Maxine Raver

The Raver family has had a connection with S.N.O.B. ever since its opening on East Bay. My parents ate there that first Saturday night and continued to do so every Saturday night for twenty years! We celebrated many family occasions with Frank Lee and his team, including my dad's one hundredth birthday party. Now we bring our own children to S.N.O.B. whenever they visit—a tradition important to all of us, not to mention the wonderful food!

—Bill and Sally Raver

RICE

．．．

HATS OFF TO GLENN Roberts, Sean Brock, and the Anson Mills crew for all the effort they've put into resurrecting heirloom grains that were practically extinct in the mid-1990s. Sean refers to it as, "Reestablishing the Carolina pantry."

We use a lot of Campbell Coxe's rice, where he grows it up in Horry County, under the name Carolina Plantation Rice. Visiting his rice field is like going back in time. You expect to see dinosaurs come lumbering out of that virile, primeval land on the edge of the Pee Dee River. It's a place that will take the cosmopolitan edge right off of your view of South Carolina.

Carolina Gold Rice

Cooking rice is all about keeping its integrity, and there are a lot of different ways to do it. The way we make it is a very old method, but it's tried and true.

Tools needed: 2-quart pot with lid

Yield: 2 cups

Ingredients:

1½ cups water

¼ teaspoon salt

1 teaspoon butter

1 cup Carolina Gold Rice

1 fresh bay leaf

Method:

- Bring water, salt, and butter to a boil in the pot.
- Add rice, stir, then cover with lid and turn heat down to low. Cook 15 minutes.
- Remove from heat, fluff, re-cover, and let sit off the heat to steam 10 minutes.

Brown Rice

Brown rice, now being grown by Jimmy Hagood at Food for the Southern Soul, is a grain we like to boil like pasta: 1 cup rice to 5 cups water with a pinch of salt, brought to a boil and simmered hard for 30 minutes, then strained, put back on the pot with a tablespoon of butter, covered, and allowed to steam another 10 minutes.

Green Farro

We've had great success with the different grains that have been coming out recently, including green farro that we get locally from Anson Mills. It's fragrant, nutty, toothy, and thoroughly wholesome.

Method:

- With the farro we'll do more of a 2½-parts-liquid to one-part-farro ratio and simmer it, cooking it for about 20 minutes until it's the texture we want and then letting it sit for 10.
- Combining the green farro with roasted roots or tender green vegetables at the last minute is a signature style of S.N.O.B.

George Cogar

 I first found S.N.O.B. through Janie Atkinson, a wonderful interior designer who was faux-finishing our walls at the same time she was doing the walls at S.N.O.B.. So we knew it was about to open, and after our first meal, we've been coming back ever since. It sounds cliché, but S.N.O.B. really is a place where everyone knows your name. This establishment speaks for itself: the food here never disappoints, it's always excellent, and you're always served with a smile.

Jill Maynard

 I started at S.N.O.B. in 1997 and was blown away that local farmers and fishermen would pull right up to the back door. The raw ingredients were beautifully displayed and eventually turned into culinary masterpieces by Chef Frank Lee and his Cuisine Commandos. Everyone was so proud to work at this unique restaurant. The vibe for the guests and employees alike was all about having a good time and enjoying fantastic food.

Dr. Mary Thornley

 Dick Elliott and Chef Frank Lee have been magnets, attracting newbies and regulars to S.N.O.B. for years. Perhaps the most special visit for me was when my son Damon and his friend David surprised me with a birthday dinner at S.N.O.B. on a busy Saturday night: Frank Lee took the time to visit with us, chat with Damon about every dish, and surprise me further with a chocolate molten dessert! I love Frank Lee!

Jim Bush

 S.N.O.B. became my favorite restaurant shortly after I moved to Charleston. It started with incredibly friendly staff, many of whom I remain friends with today. Beyond the staff, it's always been about the food. Chef Lee's ability to combine ingredients from all over the Lowcountry into amazing dishes continues to inspire. He encourages me to be adventurous and try new things. S.N.O.B. is not only one of the most innovative restaurants in Charleston; it's like home to me!

SOUTHERN SUNDAY SUPPER

SO MUCH OF WHAT we've tried to do at S.N.O.B. is to bring the civility of the Southern Sunday supper to the rhythm of the restaurant. These are some of my favorites.

Granny Mobley's Eggplant Casserole

YIELD

4-6 servings

TOOLS NEEDED

2-gallon pot, 1-quart casserole dish

Light, delicate, and full of eggplant goodness.

Ingredients

6 cups eggplant, peeled and medium-diced

2 cups water

1 teaspoon salt

1 egg

3 tablespoons onion, minced

1 teaspoon oregano

1½ tablespoons

butter, melted

½ teaspoon pepper

½ cup panko crumbs

1 cup cheddar, grated

½ cup Parmigiano-Reggiano, grated

½ teaspoon paprika

2 tomatoes, peeled and sliced thin

Method

Preheat oven to 375° and butter casserole dish.

Boil eggplant in salt and water, covered, for 5 minutes or until tender. Drain.

Beat egg and add butter, oregano, onion, salt, pepper, and panko together. Add eggplant.

Layer half of the tomato slices in casserole dish, then all eggplant, then remaining half of tomatoes.

Mix cheeses with paprika and use to top casserole.

Bake 35–40 minutes.

Collard Greens

YIELD	TOOLS NEEDED
~6 servings	2-gallon pot with lid

WE USE GREENS SO much in the S.N.O.B kitchen. They speak to the Lowcountry and to our farmers and to the rhythm of our seasons and the region, from the greens off a turnip to mustard greens or collards.

Most of us have a tendency to cook greens with a lot of bacon and season them up with vinegar, hot sauce, and sugar. That's fine. It tastes great and we do it a lot. But I would challenge the home cook to back off on all of that and try to cook the greens to the point where they're tender, seasoning them up in a minimal fashion so that you can actually taste the greens. If you don't like it, you can always add the sweet and the hot afterward.

This recipe brings the collard flavor to the palate with the bacon and vinegar complimentary in these amounts.

Ingredients

1 bunch collards, stems removed, washed, and cut into ½" ribbons

6 oz. smoked bacon, small-diced

2 cups onions, small-diced

½ cup apple cider vinegar

½ teaspoon salt

½ teaspoon pepper

2 cups water

Method

Lightly brown the bacon in the pot.

Add onions and sweat until tender over medium heat, without burning.

Add vinegar, salt, and pepper and cook 2 minutes to take the raw off the vinegar.

Add the collards and water and cook, covered, over medium-low heat for 45 minutes to 1 hour until tender, stirring often.

VARIATION

Use either mustard or turnip greens instead of collards, backing off slightly on the bacon and vinegar.

TASTES LIKE GREENS

I understand that I'm kind of in the minority when it comes to greens, and a lot of that had to do with my adopted granny, Phyllis Mobley.

Every Sunday while I was in high school, Granny Mobley's grandsons and I would go to her house for dinner and she would put out this quintessential Southern Sunday spread. If we didn't go back for seconds or thirds, she was bitterly disappointed.

She and her Jamaican maid, Viola, could cook greens that were just heavenly. Her mustard greens were unbelievable, and she didn't put a lot of stuff in them. She might have a tiny bit of bacon in there or a tiny bit of onion, but when she cooked greens, they tasted like greens. They were so supple and tender, and I've always tried to emulate that.

Dad's Spiced Rutabagas

This was my dad's favorite way to do rutabagas, letting the liquid cook down until the vinegar was almost gone, leaving this piquant, flavorful dish. With caraway seed, it's a different animal.

José de Anacleto, chef of Charleston's Restaurant Million, gave me the honor of serving Louis Latour a dish of rutabagas with pompano. Monsieur Latour enjoyed his Lowcountry repast and informed me he hadn't had rutabagas since the war. Apparently, rutabagas are feed for livestock in France. Oops ... not with caraway seeds, they're not.

Tools needed: 3-quart pot, colander

Yield: 6 servings

Ingredients:

2 pounds rutabaga, peeled and medium-diced

6 cups lightly salted water

3 tablespoons butter

¼ cup apple cider vinegar

1 teaspoon caraway seeds

2 tablespoons brown sugar

¼ teaspoon salt

1 fresh red chili pepper, seeded and sliced thin

Method:

- Boil rutabaga in pot with lightly salted water until tender, ~15 minutes, then strain into colander.

- Melt butter in pot, then add rutabagas, vinegar, caraway seeds, sugar, and salt, and cook until almost dry; stir in red chili peppers.

Scalloped Sweet Potato with Horseradish Cream

This is a recipe we did way back when that's different and simple. There's something about the acid in the horseradish, but the flavors of the two marry together in a way that brings out the sweetness of the sweet potato while adding this indiscernible dimension to it—transcending their individual tastes and creating an entirely different flavor.

Tools needed: 1-quart baking dish with lid

Yield: 4 servings

Ingredients:

4 cups sweet potatoes, peeled and sliced ⅛" thick

1 cup cream

½ cup plus 1 tablespoon prepared horseradish

1 teaspoon salt

½ teaspoon white pepper, ground

Method:

- Heat oven to 375°.

- Mix the cream with the horseradish, salt, and pepper.

- Layer the sweet potato slices in buttered casserole dish and pour cream mixture over the potatoes.

- Cover with lid and bake at 375° for 45 minutes.

House Cornbread

YIELD	TOOLS NEEDED
~3 dozen squares	9" x 11" baking pan

O
UR CORNBREAD HAS BEEN an interesting journey. Over the years, Big G has worked out a recipe for cornbread that's so tender and so rich in butter and sugar that it's more like corn cake, and our customers love it. We bake it at a fairly low temperature, which means it has to go in early and stay there, even though we're often fighting for the oven it's in. He's very particular about it and very proud, as he should be. He's perfected it.

Ingredients

2½ cups yellow cornmeal

3½ cups flour

2 tablespoons baking powder

½ teaspoon salt

¾ pound butter, melted

½ cup canola oil

1½ cups sugar

3 cups milk

3 eggs

Method

Heat oven to 325°.

Mix together the eggs, canola oil, sugar, and butter, making sure the butter has cooled a little so that it doesn't cook the eggs, and beat well.

Mix dry ingredients together and then add to the egg mixture, beating well.

Add milk and beat until all lumps are gone.

Pour into greased 9" x 11" pan and bake for 1 hour, 10 minutes or until done.

Alex and Marybeth Myers

We first met Chef Lee when we saw him filleting fish and asked our waitress a question about it. Frank came over with a Spanish mackerel and told us why he loves this much-maligned fish, then sautéed a fillet for us to try. He obviously loves his craft! From the express lunch, to the Southern Medley, carpaccio, cornbread, and shrimp and grits, to Chef Russ Moore's amazing Sunday suppers, S.N.O.B. is a treasure.

S.N.O.B. Coleslaw

YIELD

8 cups

TOOLS NEEDED

sharp knife or mandoline

WE GROW A LOT of cabbage in this state, but it's one of those vegetables that's been taken down to its lowest common denominator. We love it in soups, or **Blanching** it the same way we do all our green vegetables (*p. 72*). Reheat the blanched cabbage with butter until it relaxes and you have an excellent melted cabbage.

Ingredients

1 gallon cabbage, sliced thin

1 cup carrots, grated

¼ cup sugar

½ cup apple cider vinegar

1 cup Duke's mayonnaise

½ tablespoon celery seed

1 tablespoon salt

1 tablespoon pepper

Method

Mix together sugar, vinegar, mayo, celery seed, salt, and pepper.

Add cabbage and carrots and mix well.

Field Pea Ragout

One of those things that's almost unique to the Low country is our countless varieties of field peas.

When peas come in, we always **Blanch** them first (*p. 72*), then we either get them ready to serve or freeze. The ones we're going to serve might be seasoned with some smoked pork or added to a *mirepoix* that's been sweated down with olive oil or pork fat, adding a little bit of water or chicken stock depending on which way you want to go.

Peas marry so well with local **Carolina Gold Rice** (*p. 81*) or **Grits** (*p. 79*) that it's almost like cheating. They're so easy, full of flavor and texture, and they speak so much to our region.

Tools needed: 2-gallon pot

Yield: ~6 cups

Ingredients:

2 oz. butter

1 cup onion, small-diced

1 cup carrot, small-diced

1 cup celery, small-diced

2 cups **Chicken Stock** (*p. 171*) (or water)

1 teaspoon salt

½ teaspoon pepper

4 cups fresh field peas, **Blanched** (*p. 72*)

1 teaspoon fresh thyme

Method:

- Melt butter.
- Add vegetables and sauté until soft.
- Add field peas and chicken stock (or water), and season with salt and pepper.
- Cook over low heat until peas are tender and most of the liquid is absorbed, ~20–30 minutes.
- Remove from heat and cool until ready to serve

Country-Style Yellow Squash

YIELD	TOOLS NEEDED
~4 servings	2-gallon pot with lid, potato masher

YOU SEE COUNTRY-STYLE YELLOW squash on the menus at S.N.O.B. a lot, and that recipe is one that I got from my wife, Robin. When yellow squash comes in, it comes in. There's squash everywhere. What do you do with all that squash? So she taught me how to make it country style, cooking the squash down so that the flavors intensify, and doing it quickly so that it stays bright yellow and keeps that wonderful sweetness.

When making country-style squash:

- The squash has to be a great quality to start with. It can't be too old, bruised, or damaged, or it will take on a brownish tinge.

- You need to watch it when it first gets going because it's easy to scorch.

- Don't cook it too long and slowly, either, because it will lose its brilliant yellow color.

When you start with something good, it's hard to screw it up. But you have to practice. You have to do it properly and you have to develop the proper technique.

Ingredients

4 tablespoons butter

2 cups onion, small-diced

5 pounds small, unblemished yellow squash, small-diced

2 teaspoons salt

½ teaspoon pepper

1 cup water

Method

Heat all ingredients over high heat for 5–10 minutes, until squash gives up juice.

Using a potato masher, mash until evenly mashed and uniformly bright yellow.

Turn to medium and cook, stirring frequently to avoid scorching, until squash juices have reduced, intensifying the flavor.

Stewed Okra and Tomatoes

YIELD

2–3 servings

TOOLS NEEDED

2-quart nonreactive pot

ASTANDARD AT SUNDAY LUNCH, this is a simple prep that lets the tomatoes and okra do the talking. Gotta have some rice for this one.

Ingredients

2 cups onion, medium-diced

4 cups tomatoes, peeled and medium-diced

2 tablespoons olive oil

1 tablespoon tomato paste

1 teaspoon salt

1 tablespoon sugar

4 cups okra, medium slice

½ teaspoon pepper

½ teaspoon Tabasco

1 batch **Carolina Gold Rice** (P. 81)

Method

Sweat onions in oil and salt, then add sugar, tomatoes, and tomato paste.

Bring to a simmer, add the okra, and simmer 15 minutes.

Finish with pepper and Tabasco.

Okra Pilaf

This is an example of rhythm of service and *mise en place*. We have our rice freshly cooked, just barely to the side of being done. The combination of the okra, bell pepper, and ham could be replaced with diced tomatoes and basil; or roasted fennel and butternut squash; or roasted chicken, sausage, and bell pepper; or bacon, field peas, and green onion ...

Tools needed: skillet

Yield: 4 servings

Ingredients:

½ cup onion, diced

½ cup red bell pepper, medium-diced

¼ cup country ham, medium-diced

1 cup **Carolina Gold Rice**, cooked (*p. 81*)

1 cup **Chicken Stock** (*p. 171*) or water

12 small okra, stemmed

1 tablespoon olive oil

1 tablespoon parsley, medium-diced

salt

pepper

Method:

- Heat the olive oil and ham in skillet, then add bell pepper and onion and sweat.

- Add rice, okra, and ½ cup stock (or water). Cover and cook gently for rice to plump and okra to steam *al dente*. Add additional stock as needed.

- Season and stir in parsley. Boom! Pilaf with okra *al dente* in less than 10 minutes.

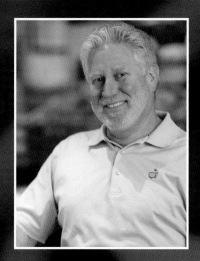

Steve Connor

First guest to make 1,000 reservations

The bar and service staff are friendly, knowledgeable, and professional. Frequently dining at the Chef's table, we've had the opportunity to interact with the great staff, getting to know each other and becoming more than a customer. We are friends, and my wife, Tami, and I feel like we are truly members of the S.N.O.B. family! S.N.O.B. is special, and they make us feel special!

Risotto with Squash Blossoms

YIELD	TOOLS NEEDED
2 servings	2-quart pot

PEOPLE LOVE RISOTTO, BUT it's been terribly abused over the years. And we've probably abused it, too. People think risotto is a vehicle for enormous amounts of butter and cheese ... not exactly, although it can be.

If you want a good risotto, you need that short-grain, starchy rice so you can develop the starch in it, and you need to make it *a la minute*. It's hard to get right, but when you do, it's fantastic.

Ingredients

2 tablespoons Arborio rice

1 tablespoon onion, minced

2 teaspoons butter

8 oz. **Chicken Stock** (P. 171)

2 tablespoons Parmigiano-Reggiano, grated

1 tablespoon **Cooked Corn** (P. 78)

6 squash blossoms, medium-diced

salt

pepper

Method

Lightly brown onion and rice in 1 teaspoon butter.

Add chicken stock 2 oz. at a time, stirring constantly, until rice is plump and *al dente*, ~12 minutes.

Remove pot from heat and add corn, remaining butter, and cheese. Salt and pepper to taste.

Add squash blossoms and serve immediately.

Big G's Dried White Limas

YIELD

12-14 servings

TOOLS NEEDED

2-gallon pot with lid

BIG G STARTED COOKING staff meals once a week in about 2000 or 2001, and when he does it, he does it with a passion.

He'll cook tasty things like chicken wings with three different barbecue sauces, or an incredibly rich, cheesy pasta. One winter, many years back, he started doing dried white limas with the neck bone and pig tail stock. It was a deep-down Southern dish, and we liked it so much that we worked out a recipe for it, serving it on the menu with pork chop or baked chicken, or pairing the limas with an **Okra Pilaf** (*p. 93*).

Ingredients

2 pounds dried white lima beans, large

1 gallon water

2 cups onion, small-diced

1 cup celery, small-diced

1 jalapeño, seeded and small-diced

2 teaspoons salt

2 teaspoons pepper

½ cup olive oil

6 cups **Neck Bone, Ham Hock, Pig Tail Stock** (*p. 172*)

2 cups meat from neck bone, ham hock, pig tail stock, medium-diced

Method

Rinse and pick over beans, removing any dirt, rocks, etc.

Put beans in a pot with water, bring to a boil and boil ~2 minutes.

Cover and let sit an hour, then strain and rinse.

Clean out the pot and add olive oil, celery, onions, jalapeño, and salt, cooking until tender.

Add the lima beans and neck bone stock.

Simmer, covered, over low heat ~45 minutes to 1 hour, cooking gently so as not to break up the beans.

Cook until tender, then stir in pepper and the medium-diced meat from the stock.

Merrill Benfield

For years, I had this routine with former S.N.O.B. owner, Dick Elliott. I would come in right at 11:30 a.m., take my regular seat at the bar, and divide up that day's copy of *The Wall Street Journal*. Dick would get the first two sections, I'd read the rest, and then we'd switch. Neither of us said a word, and this went on for years! Later, when Dick told me the name of his new restaurant was going to be "High Cotton," it gave me great pride to gift him with my British sports car's license plate that for years featured the name of my father's boat, *High Cotton*. I'm told that plate became a permanent fixture on his desk.

And I still love that, too this day, I don't have to order steak from Frank. I just look back at him in the kitchen, and he holds his fingers apart as thick as he thinks I'll like my steak. I either nod or sign back with a slight adjustment.

S.N.O.B. is where my heart is and for more than 20 years it has been my home, my kitchen, and my extended family.

Frances Bramlett

general manager, 1995–2001

I count the years I spent at S.N.O.B. as some of the best of my life, professionally and personally. I was hired as director of operations, but shortly after my arrival, I was asked to fill in as interim general manager for a "few weeks." Those few weeks turned into six years! From the moment I walked in the door, I knew I belonged. Every dishwasher, line cook, server assistant, server, bartender, hostess—no one settled for second best. There was so much pride of place, each striving for excellence every single day. Our customers were guests in our home. My partners—Dick Elliott, David Marconi, and Frank Lee—created a synergy that was sterling and rare; it was a magic time for all of us.

THE DINER

WE'RE KNOWN FOR OUR Lunch Express. It's our businessman's lunch: soup or salad, main course, and either coffee, tea, or soda. It's quick and affordable, and for sixteen years we kept the price under ten dollars.

This is where the restaurant takes on the personality of a diner, and because the Lunch Express changes every day, it gives us the freedom to be very eclectic within the rhythm of *mise en place*. We could cook classics like meatloaf or egg foo young, burritos or ramen noodle bowls, or beef bourguignon.

It's fun for us, and it's fun for the customers, because they never know what the Lunch Express is going to be from day to day. What they *do* know is that it's going to be affordable, quick, and cooked with the same quality and integrity that we put into everything we do at S.N.O.B.

No you don't get the recipe for this!

If you want it call Arnold's Country
Kitchen in Nashville like I DID

thanks Arnold's!

Shrimp Creole

YIELD	TOOLS NEEDED
4 servings	2-gallon nonreactive pot, skillet

ONE OF MY CLEAREST childhood memories is of the shrimp creole served during the church socials at my aunt's church on Pawley's Island—a small, one-room chapel with an ancient graveyard that sat right next to the Waccamaw River under a thicket of moss-covered trees. In the heat of summer there was the salt breeze blowing in from the river and the grasshoppers endlessly droning. It was sublime.

It was my aunt's neighbor, Mr. King, who made the Shrimp Creole. Mr. King was the owner of King's Funland on Pawley's, and he must have been of Irish decent because he had flaming red hair and was so big that he used the inner-tube from a tractor to float around in the ocean.

I remember him standing over that giant cowboy cauldron of creole—baggy pants, shirtless, a red apron draped around his waist and sweat just pouring off of him as he stirred away with a big wooden paddle. He'd make it with local shrimp and serve it over long-grain Horry County rice from Marlow's or Lachicotte's.

Shrimp creole is another one of those things that's been abused; taken down to the lowest level. When we make it, we make it Lowcountry-style with the trinity and tomatoes, making our own shrimp stock from the shells and heads to moisten it.

Ingredients

2 cups yellow onion, medium-diced

2 cups bell pepper, medium-diced

2 cups celery, medium-diced

¼ teaspoon garlic, mashed

4 cups tomatoes, peeled, seeded, and medium-diced

2 cups Shrimp Stock (*p. 172*)

1 tablespoon Worcestershire

1 teaspoon Tabasco

2 tablespoons sugar

1 teaspoon salt

3 tablespoons olive oil

1 teaspoon pepper

2 tablespoons fresh thyme, medium-diced

2 bay leaves

3 pounds shrimp, peeled and deveined

1 tablespoon garlic, minced

4 tablespoons butter

1 batch Carolina Gold Rice (*p. 81*)

Method

In pot, sweat down vegetables (not tomatoes) with olive oil, salt, and pepper until tender.

Add tomatoes and herbs and simmer 5 minutes until tomatoes render their juices.

Add stock and seasonings, then simmer another 5 minutes to marry the flavors.

Sautee shrimp in garlic and butter for ~3 minutes or until pink and cooked through.

Serve with rice.

Salmon Croquettes

This is another dish like the fried chicken livers that I thought would never sell—wrong again! The croquettes are simple cakes of salmon mixed with a little bit of egg and Panko and then enriched with sour cream, fresh dill, and capers. A good example of respect: using up all of the critter and making it taste great!

Tools needed: skillet

Yield: 4 servings

Ingredients:

4 tablespoons sour cream

1 egg

1 pound raw salmon, minced

2 tablespoons lemon juice

½ teaspoon salt

1 tablespoon capers, medium-diced (reserve some juice)

4 dashes Tabasco

1 cup Panko, divided

2 tablespoons fresh dill

½ cup parsley

¼ cup red onion, small-diced

olive oil or butter, for pan frying

Method:

- Beat egg with sour cream and add salmon.
- Reserve ½ cup Panko and add all remaining ingredients, mixing well.
- Refrigerate at least one hour.
- Form into four 5-oz. cakes, coat with reserved breadcrumbs, and pan fry in olive oil or butter.

Beef Stew with Green Olives

YIELD

6-8 servings

TOOLS NEEDED

2-gallon oven-safe pot with lid

WHEN WE WERE GETTING local beef from Stevenson Place Farms up in Greenwood, South Carolina—owned by my dermatologist and great customer, Dr. Stephanie Smith-Phillips—we'd buy just about whatever they had, and a lot of times what they had was beef shank or brisket or chuck. Those shanks, especially, were really tough, so we'd have to take our time slow-braising them.

The great thing about braising is that you're melting tough tendons and ligaments and nerves and fat. It makes a terrific braising jus, and the beef turns out tender and unctuous.

For our recipe, we finish it with green olives and pearl onions and little bright vegetables, which creates that harmonic dissonance between the rich, unctuous stew and the vividly fresh vegetables.

It's a wonderful dish and one that takes us two days to make, but it suits our rhythm of using things up and turning out something pleasing and balanced.

Ingredients

2 pounds stew beef, cut into 2" cubes

2 teaspoons salt

2 teaspoons pepper

1 cup flour

1 cup olive oil

2 cups each of onion, carrot, and celery, medium-diced

1 cup red wine

3 cups tomato, diced, peeled, and seeded

3 cups chicken stock

2 tablespoons thyme, medium-diced

4 tablespoons garlic, minced

½ cup green olives, sliced and rinsed

Method

Preheat oven to 350°.

Heat olive oil in pot.

Season meat with salt and pepper, dredge in flour, and sear in hot oil.

Remove meat and set aside. Pour off excess oil and sweat the onion, carrot, and celery.

Add meat back in and sprinkle with 2 tablespoons of flour to make a *roux*.

Add red wine, tomatoes, stock, herbs, and garlic.

Bring to a bubble, cover, and bake in oven 1 hour.

Check for tenderness (if meat is tougher, it may take longer). When tender, remove from oven, add olives, and let rest, covered, for 30 minutes before serving.

Meatloaf

YIELD	TOOLS NEEDED
6-8 servings	9" x 5" loaf pan

OUR MEATLOAF IS ANOTHER part of our rhythm—a way we use the whole critter up. We use Celeste Albers' ground beef and feature caraway and fennel seeds, wrapping the loaf in bacon, glazing it with **Black Jack BBQ Sauce** (*p. 163*), and serving it with a **Madeira Sauce** (*p. 175*) and a **Blanched** (*p. 72*) green vegetable.

Many more of our guests like meatloaf for lunch more than a *torchon* of foie gras. Who knew? It's another dish I didn't think would sell but turned out to be incredibly popular. And it gives me joy to make something that our patrons love to eat.

Ingredients

1 pound tenderloin scraps, ground

1 egg

¼ cup Panko

½ cup yellow onion

½ cup red bell pepper

1 tablespoon olive oil

1 teaspoon fennel seeds

½ teaspoon red pepper flakes

1 teaspoon caraway

½ teaspoon pepper

1 teaspoon salt

3 tablespoons ketchup

8–10 slices bacon

Method

Preheat oven to 325°.

Dice bell pepper and onions, sweat in olive oil, and chill to room temperature.

Grind fennel, pepper, and caraway.

Mix all ingredients (except bacon) well.

Line loaf pan with bacon, fill with meatloaf mix, and fold bacon ends over top.

Bake 1 hour or until internal temperature reaches 160°.

"EXCUSE ME, SIR. IS THAT MEATLOAF?"

When we opened in 1993, we had a waiter at S.N.O.B. named John Kelly. He was in his late 60s then—a distinguished gentleman of the old school who just knew service backward and forward—but wasn't really up-to-date on popular culture.

One day, a customer seated at one of Mr. Kelly's stations noticed another one of our longtime patrons, who happened to be a rather rotund fellow with long blonde hair and who bore a striking resemblance to the performer, Meatloaf.

When Mr. Kelly brought out the crab-stuffed flounder with shrimp that his customer had ordered, the customer beckoned Mr. Kelly closer, gestured toward the blonde patron, and said, "Excuse me, sir. Is that Meatloaf?"

Mr. Kelly got this kind of odd look on his face, looked down at the plate, and said, "No sir, this is crab-stuffed flounder." He had no idea who Meatloaf was.

To this day, whenever I think of crab-stuffed flounder, I think of that story and it still cracks me up.

Pad Thai

YIELD	TOOLS NEEDED
1 serving	wok

WHEN I WAS A cook coming up in Chicago, I worked six days a week with Mondays off. Since my wife worked during the day, that became my day to go out and do laundry, buy a big cigar, and get lunch by myself. We didn't have a lot back then—to the point where we got excited if Mom sent a care package with Milanos and toilet paper in it—so I had to look for inexpensive places to have a good lunch.

Chicago being a city with ethnic neighborhoods, I was able to find a good restaurant called Thai Star where I could get a big bowl of pad Thai with lots of condiments for about $3.50. Now, that's a lunch.

In early 1990s Charleston, pad Thai wasn't available, so I put it on the menu at S.N.O.B. I had no idea how to cook it, but I did some research and we managed to do a solid version of it.

There were people, though, who would harass me and say, "This isn't Southern food." So I'd use some artistic license and say, "Well, we have a rich history in rice and these are rice noodles. Pork and shrimp are big in our culture, and those are in there, too. Peanuts are about as Southern as you get and this dish has medium-diced peanuts on it, so there you go."

Ingredients

- ~2 oz. olive oil
- 3 oz. raw pork loin, sliced
- ½ cup green onions
- ~5 shrimp, peeled and deveined
- 2 cups soaked rice noodles, drained
- 4 oz. **Pad Thai Juice** (recipe adjacent)
- ¼ teaspoon medium-diced garlic
- 1 egg
- 1 cup mung beans
- 2 lime wedges
- 1 teaspoon garlic chili paste
- ¼ bunch cilantro
- 1 oz. peanuts

PAD THAI JUICE:
- 1 cup white vinegar
- ½ cup fish sauce
- ½ cup sugar
- ¼ cup tamarind juice
- 1 tablespoon paprika

Method

Make pad Thai juice, blending all ingredients until sugar dissolves.

Heat oil and add pork, searing on one side.

Add noodles, garlic, and pad Thai juice.

Cook 2 minutes or until noodles soak up juice.

Add shrimp and sauté until half-done.

Fry egg on side of wok until sunny-side up, then toss with noodle mix.

Wait 20 seconds, then stir in mung beans and green onion.

Pour in bowl and garnish with garlic chili paste, cilantro, squeeze of one lime wedge, placing other lime wedge on bowl rim. Sprinkle peanuts on top.

Kaye and Johnny Wallace

Frank was doing farm-to-table long before anyone else, working with the farmers on Wadmalaw and the local fishermen. We loved to come in just to try whatever fresh vegetables came in that day. It was so much fun watching that crazy guy in his chili hat and pants work his magic in the kitchen, and no matter what, the food always came out great. To this day, he makes the best pad Thai in Charleston.

MEDIUM PLATES

AS CUISINE DEVELOPS, A balance falls into place. There's a balance in the offerings between meat and vegetarian, exotic and local, crisp and soft, sour and sweet, dark and light. It's a juxtaposition of the senses that ultimately provides our guests with honest cooking that takes no shortcuts, that emphasizes quality, integrity, and consistency with every bite. This balance has made S.N.O.B. a place where you could dine fifty times a year and never have the same dish twice. People are looking for new choices all the time, and our menu reflects that desire. You can dine small or large, light or heavy, create a multi-course dining experience or have a light meal and go. Our medium plates are a reflection of that mentality, of providing our customers with choices and balance, quality and variety.

Kitty Robinson

S.N.O.B. is one of my very favorite restaurants!

As a lunchtime regular, I am humbled and most appreciative that every time I walk in the front door, I am greeted by name with an automatic smile from whomever is behind the reception desk.

While I have many favorites, including the beautiful and deliciously fresh salads and daily lunch specials, I most often defer to my first choice: the irresistible grilled Southern Medley! Much of the menu is local, making each choice all the more appreciated, and the look of every plate resembles the work of an artist. The entire experience is magical!

Grilled Southern Medley

YIELD	TOOLS NEEDED
1 serving	grill or grill pan, skillet

THIS IS ANOTHER DISH that's been on the S.N.O.B. menu since we opened, and it's one we serve all year long. That's part of the freedom, the artistic license that we have. It's called Southern Medley because it's all big-time South Carolina ingredients, though we do it with a Mediterranean flair.

Ingredients

1, 6–8-oz. boneless skinless chicken breast

1 each zucchini, tomato, eggplant, sliced ½"- ¾" thick

2, 1-oz. balls local goat cheese

Calabash Crumbs *(p. 123)* and flour to coat balls

2 tablespoons Parmigiano-Reggiano, grated

2–3 leaves fresh basil, chiffonade

1 egg plus 2 tablespoons water, blended

GARNISH WITH:

Basil Pesto *(p. 166)*

Balsamic Vinaigrette *(p. 176)*

Method

Rub your chicken breast in a blend of olive oil, crushed red pepper, dried basil, oregano, salt, and pepper.

Brush cut vegetables with olive oil, season with salt and pepper.

Grill all, starting with chicken and eggplant and throwing on zucchini and tomato last.

Beef Carpaccio

WE'VE HAD THE BEEF carpaccio on the S.N.O.B. menu since day one, and I'd never made it until the day we opened. I had no idea how to do it, but we figured it out and over the years it's evolved into this lovely light lunch. The trick is in freezing the meat first, slicing it micro-thin on a commercial deli slicer, then refreezing it in single layers until ready to eat.

Roll goat cheese in 1 oz. balls, dip in flour, then egg wash, and roll in **Calabash Crumbs** (*p. 123*). Pan fry in olive oil.

Put 1 tablespoon **Basil Pesto** on plate. Arrange tomato at 12 o'clock, eggplant in the middle, and zucchini at 6 o'clock.

Split thick side of chicken breast so it acts as feet, standing it on top of the eggplant. Strew goat balls around and drizzle with **Balsamic Vinaigrette**, parmesan cheese, and a chiffonade of basil.

Method

Clean a beef eye of round free of sinew and freeze it in manageable chunks that fit on a heavy-duty deli slicer.

Slice it super thin on the slicer, layering 3 oz. of the meat on the plate and adding a zigzag of Dijonnaise and **Red Wine Vinaigrette** (*p. 176*), garnishing with capers, cornichons, a small salad, and toast.

Medium Plates

Palmetto Pigeon

YIELD	TOOLS NEEDED
2 servings	skillet

SQUAB, OR YOUNG PIGEON, has always been one of my favorite birds, and when I lived in Chicago and DC, the pigeon was king. We sold tons of it. It's tender and it has this red meat that's succulent and flavorful, like a big dove.

No one in Charleston was selling pigeon, even though we've had the family-owned Palmetto Pigeon Plant up in Sumter since the 1920s. Every week they sent us fresh pigeon and I became a man on a mission. In the same way that I tried to become the Tamale King of Charleston when we first opened, I tried to introduce people to the pleasures of pigeon.

For fourteen years, I beat my head against the wall: pigeon, pigeon, sell the pigeon. At any special event, I'd do pigeon. It's a local prod-uct and the perfect complement to so many things—from truffles, foie gras, and a great burgundy to simply corn and rice. One way we like to serve it is with a **Sherry Wine Reduction** (*P. 175*) and **Risotto with Squash Blossoms** (*P. 94*). Have a little seafood appetizer, a glass of white wine for the appetizer, and a red wine with the pigeon, and man, you're done. That's a classy meal!

But not everyone dines like I do, and ultimately, you have to respect your clients. That's where you have your balance, and I had to find that balance between what got my rocks off as a chef and what clients want to pay for. Eventually we took the squab off the menu and replaced it with quail from Manchester Farms in Dalzell, South Carolina, and it sold about seven times better than the pigeon.

Ingredients

2 squab breasts, boneless with skin on

pinch salt

pinch pepper

pinch ground star anise

1 teaspoon canola oil

Method

Trim excess fat from squab breast and season lightly with salt, pepper, and star anise.

Heat oil in skillet until hot, then sear breast skin-side down ~2 minutes, then flip and sear flesh side 30 seconds to 1 minute, rare to mid-rare.

Let rest skin-side down in a warm place for several minutes before serving.

Squash
Blossom
Risotto

Carolina Quail

MALCOLM HUDSON WAS ONE of the first people to buy quail from Bill Odom at Manchester Farms when he got started in the late 1970s. He had this small place next to Shaw Air Force Base in Sumter, South Carolina, and I always had a great relationship with him. Over the years, Manchester Farms has been supportive of the Charleston restaurant scene, donating quail to almost every fundraising event you could imagine. Their phi-losophy and attitude of generosity is a great example of the collaborative culinary community we have in Charleston.

We've had several different recipes for quail over the years, and always the challenge is that one's not enough but two is too many. So we'll stuff it with **Lemon Sausage** (*p. 69*) to give it a bit more oomph, and pair that with **Plum Glaze** (*p. 167*), field peas, and mustard greens.

Quail Method

Fatten boned quail with 4oz. **Lemon Sausage** (*p. 69*) or **Chicken Mousse** (*p. 67*), wrap in bacon, and brown in a hot pan.

Finish in 375° oven until internal temperature reaches 150.

Bobby Collins

Frank Lee channels the toil from the hands of local farmers and growers

> ... to his heart,
> to his hands,
> onto our plates,
> and into our souls.

Frank doesn't feed us—he nurtures us.

"How many countless restaurant-service professionals has David Marconi taught over the years? No one really knows the exact figure, but David's Army is now spread all over Charleston area restaurants and has likely played a significant role in Charleston being voted the number-one destination city on the planet for who-knows-how-many years in a row.

In 2008, when the Great Recession was tightening its grip and all of us were finding ways to cut budgets and spending, there was a contrarian voice, a true leader. As chair of the Charleston Metro Chamber that year, my concerns were no different. Concerned our fund-raising efforts would fall woefully short, we too were looking at ways of drastically reducing budgets and spending. Would we fall 15 percent, 20 percent, 30 percent? No one knew for sure. Enter Dick Elliott, who agreed to help this no-so-confident chair by leading the Total Resource Campaign that year ... but only on one condition: we would set a goal one dollar higher than raised the previous year. Gulp. Well, of course we exceeded the goal, even in 2008. And all of us who worked shoulder to shoulder with Dick during the campaign learned a valuable lifelong lesson: If we cave in by cutting our goals, then we are doomed before we begin. We may not make it, but we mustn't give in before we begin, or we will surely fail!

I am grateful for having personally experienced the nurturing, been on the receiving end of world-class hospitality, and learned valuable lessons on leadership— particularly from such a group of mavericks!"

Dave's Clams with Roasted Garlic Cream

YIELD	TOOLS NEEDED
1 servings	small casserole dish with lid, 2-quart pot, 10" nonreactive skillet with lid, whisk

AS A CHILD, I didn't have the skill of my brother, Chris, or the talent of our legendary cousin, Cameron, when it came to catching large fish at Pawley's Island. I found great delight and satisfaction, however, in catching clams in a secret, sandy creek where I could retreat and dig with my fingers and toes. Like me, my kids have inherited my way of finding clams with ease.

This is a recipe that S.N.O.B. chef Russ Moore came up with. He always uses clams from Clammer Dave on Isle of Palms, which are very clean and tender.

Ingredients

12 littleneck clams

½ cup white wine

¼ cup **Garlic Cream** (recipe below)

1 tablespoon parsley, medium-diced

1 teaspoon butter

1 squeeze lemon

Garlic Cream (makes 1½ cups):

5 garlic heads, top cut off

½ teaspoon salt

4 tablespoons olive oil

2 tablespoons water

¼ cup white wine

¾ cup cream

2 bay leaves

Method

For Garlic Cream:

Preheat oven to 375°. Sprinkle garlic heads with salt and olive oil, add water, and bake, covered, 1 hour.

Allow to cool, covered, for 30 minutes, then squeeze out the soft, fragrant, golden cloves, and mash (should make ~½ cup).

Combine roasted garlic, cream, white wine, and bay leaves.

Bring to a simmer, whisking to incorporate garlic, for 10 minutes. Remove bay leaves and reserve.

For Clams:

Cook clams in skillet with wine, covered, over high heat, removing clams to serving dish as they open (~5 minutes).

Add ¼ cup garlic cream to remaining clam jus in skillet and bring to a bubble.

Add parsley and lemon, swirl in butter, and pour over clams.

Serve with hot, crusty, dense bread to sop up the broth.

Miss Daisy's Clam Hash

This is a simple breakfast dish that I learned years ago from Miss Daisy Smalls, a Gullah chef who worked for my great aunt, Arnie Childs, when I was a kid. I absorbed a tremendous amount from Miss Daisy, who always cooked direct, seasonal cuisine.

One of the tricks to her dish is to use the slightly salty juice from fresh clams, which you can only get by hand-shucking.

Tools needed: cast-iron skillet

Yield: 4 servings

Ingredients:

12–16 good-sized clams

8 slices bacon

1 medium onion, medium-diced

6–8 saltine crackers

2 large tablespoons parsley, medium-diced

Method:

- Soak clams in icy water. Scrub the shells and clean the clams of any muddy parts.
- Over a large bowl, carefully shuck the clams. *(NOTE: I use a sharp knife and a glove made from inner-tubes, which came in handy when Vivian Howard prepared this dish with me on* A Chef's Life*).*
- Separate the clams from the liquid, removing any little pieces of shell from the shucking. Strain and reserve juice. Chop the clams.
- Crisp the bacon, then remove and reserve bacon. Pour off most of the fat and add the onion, cooking until tender.
- Add the diced clams and juice. Bring to a quick simmer.
- Crumble the saltines in the hash to thicken– remove from heat.
- Right before serving, add the diced parsley and crumble the bacon on top.
- Daisy would serve the hash over stone ground whole **Grits** *(p. 79)* with soft scrambled eggs and sliced tomato.

MAIN COURSES

AT S.N.O.B., WE ALWAYS give you the opportunity to eat large or small. This is your chance to eat large with several of our customers' favorites.

SEAFOOD

SEAFOOD DISHES HAVE ALWAYS been popular at S.N.O.B. As with all our dishes, we try to use local as much as possible, but that's another thing that's interesting about Charleston. We have an excellent small fishing fleet that continues to grow, but sometimes we have to get our grouper from the Gulf Coast of Florida or Louisiana, off the south coast of Jacksonville or North Carolina toward the Chesapeake. I have no qualms with buying quality fish from quality suppliers like Crosby's Seafood or Lowcountry Shellfish, especially if it's from our Southeastern region. For me, they're all the same ecosystem.

I'm not a fanatic. We do our part, but our main job is to get great product and use our technique to make it appealing and attractive to our customers so that they can be nourished and feel good. If we can do that in a sustainable, green, local manner, all the better. But sometimes you can't. That's not our philosophy. Our goal is to make people feel good.

Hog nose snapper

A WORD ON AQUACULTURE

We're not going to be able to feed the world without aquaculture; we just need to find the cleanest, smartest, more ecological way of doing it to produce a quality, healthy product. When it's done right, I'm a fan.

We've had shrimp farms here in South Carolina and still do. We have excellent catfish farms all over the place and barramundi farms in western Massachusetts that are getting high marks for their production and cleanliness.

It's an industry that's growing because we need it. It goes back to the importance of balance and rhythm. We can't live without the industrial farms, so it makes sense to do them in a manner that's ecologically sound—that is smarter, better, cleaner, and more health-oriented.

So let's find a way that does make sense. Advocate for the small and local, but advocate for improving on the large scale, as well.

Old-School Grouper

YIELD	TOOLS NEEDED
4 servings	skillet, grill or grill pan (optional)

BACK IN THE '80S, grouper was pretty much looked on as something you would catch, cut into chunks, roll in buttermilk and cornmeal, and deep fry. I'm not saying that's not a delicious dish and a great way to go, but in those days, grouper didn't have the panache that it does now.

When we began running grouper, we tried to keep it simple and fresh and bright while giving people choices. We got it in whole, using the excess to make things like the Fish Mousse or **Fish Stock** (*p. 172*).

It was an old-school dish that reflected our style because it was light and we didn't serve it with an obligatory starch and vegetable. By keeping it simple, it left people free to order a starch if they wanted one, or to save room for an appetizer or dessert.

Ingredients

4, 6-oz. grouper filets, lightly seasoned with salt and pepper

2 cups **Calabash Crumbs** (*p. 123*)

canola oil or clarified butter

1 batch **Marinated Cucumbers** (*p. 183*)

1 batch **Shallot Butter Sauce** (*p. 165*)

2 heaping teaspoons whole-grain mustard

1 tablespoon fresh dill, rough-diced

1–2 tomatoes, thick-sliced

Method

Dredge grouper filets in calabash crumbs and sauté with oil or butter in pan, flipping over when light brown.

Finish in 400° oven until fish is almost done, ~5 minutes, then smear with mustard and place back in oven for 1–2 minutes to glaze the mustard.

Brush tomato slices lightly with oil and get hot.

Serve over tomato and top with marinated cucumbers, shallot butter sauce, and diced dill.

yes, we released this one

Spottail Bass with a Sauté of Green Vegetables

The spottail, also known as red drum, is at the heart of coastal Carolina surf fishing. As a sport, red drum fishing takes on almost mythical dimensions: the deserted sea island, late-night secret spots, epic battles with 40- to 60-pound crafty giants, and the wholesale slaughter brought on by Chef Prudhomme's immensely popular "blackened redfish." The spottail is one of the most sought-after—and, therefore, now most endangered—fish in our surf. Strict rules apply to the size of fish and how many can be kept, and any fisherman worth his salt is proud to abide by these restrictions. I have heard of easy catches in the creeks, but in the surf, these smart bronzed spottails can snap a line or throw a hook quickly, leaving a bewildered, disappointed, and hungry fisherman behind.

A 23" spottail will feed 4 people nicely. The meat is not only plentiful but also succulent and sweeter than a black drum.

The home cook can enjoy local spottails, but restaurants are restricted from serving locally caught fish.

Tools needed: skillet, paper bag

Yield: 4–6 servings

Ingredients*:

4, 6–8-oz. spottail filets, skinned

16 asparagus, ~4" long

20 tiny green beans, blanched

½ cup green peas

12 snow pea pods

4 tablespoons butter

2 tablespoons fresh chives

3–4 oz. white wine

2 lemons, cut into wedges

1 cup **Calabash Crumbs** (*p. 123*)

salt

pepper

¼ cup olive oil

Method:

- Heat oil until almost smoking.
- Salt and pepper the filets, then shake in a bag with calabash crumbs.
- Shake off excess mix and fry until golden brown and fish is tender.
- Drain on a previously read newspaper.
- Wipe the pan out, then toss in all vegetables along with 1 tablespoon butter and salt to taste. Let it get hot, then add wine and cook until *al dente*.
- Swirl in remaining butter, then add chives and salt and pepper to taste.
- Mound the vegetables in the middle of the plate, place fish on top, and spoon the buttery chive sauce over the fish. Serve with lemons.

My kids like the spottail with a homemade tartar sauce, mashed potatoes, green beans, and lots of lemons and Tabasco (so do I).

Crab-Stuffed Flounder

YIELD	TOOLS NEEDED
4 servings	meat mallet, skillet

CRAB-STUFFED FLOUNDER IS A quintessentially Low-country dish. Traditionally, the stuffed flounder is one filet down, a layer of deviled crab, and another filet over the top. Instead, we took these iconic South Carolina ingredients and treated them with the *paupiette* technique, topping it with two Cajun-spiced shrimp and serving it with the sauce for our **Shrimp Creole** (*p. 100*). Later on, we graduated to serving it with a **Shiitake Mushroom Butter** (*p. 165*), but it was always a kind of tongue-in-cheek seafood platter: flounder, crab, and shrimp served in two sizes.

It was an incredibly popular dish and one we had for ten years until it became so defining that we had to kill it to move forward.

Ingredients

4, 6-oz. filets of flounder, skinned

8 oz. **Deviled Crab** (2 oz.+ per flounder) (*p. 139*)

1 cup **Calabash Crumbs** (*p. 123*)

¼ cup canola oil

1 batch **Shiitake Mushroom Butter** (*p. 165*)

salt

pepper

Method

Heat oven to 400°.

Split each flounder filet lengthwise, trimming away any bones.

Lay the filet on a cutting board, skin-side up, and lightly flatten with the side of a meat mallet.

Season with salt and pepper.

Spread 2 oz.+ **Deviled Crab** on the fish and gently roll from tail to head, forming the roulade with your hand, and then stuff some more deviled crab in the ends ... yeah.

Roll the flounder in your breadcrumbs of choice, then brown flounder in oil, seam-side down first, then all over.

Bake, rolling once, for 10–15 minutes or until internal temperature reaches 145°.

Calabash Crumbs

This mixture is from Calabash in the Pawley's Island area—considered to be the fried-seafood capital of South Carolina. Fresh, local seafood fried in clean oil is magnificent.

  2 cups cracker meal

  ½ cup flour

  1 tablespoon salt

  1 teaspoon pepper

Gluten-Free Calabash Crumbs

Matthew Niessner, Chef of Hall's Chophouse, turned me onto this mixture and it works great, also. The dynamics remain the same—fresh and clean.

  1 cup rice flour

  1 cup corn flour

  1 teaspoon Cajun spice

Triggerfish

YIELD	TOOLS NEEDED
2-4 servings	skillet

A LOCAL FISH THAT WE'VE been serving since S.N.O.B. opened in the early '90s and one that I've been serving since the late '80s, is triggerfish. It's a wonderful local fish that's only gained traction in recent years. When guests order it, I love asking them how they would describe it because triggerfish is unique. It has a firmness and natural sweetness to it. It's juicy, too, with a texture either like that of a turbo or dover sole. It's one of our best local fish and it applies itself well to the grill.

Ingredients

2, 10-oz. triggerfish filets, skinned and boned

2 oz. olive oil

salt

pepper

Method

Heat 1 oz. olive oil until smoking.

Coat filet with oil and cook in hot skillet until browned, ~3 to 4 minutes.

Flip the fish, cook another minute, and remove pan from heat, letting the fish passively finish cooking in the pan for ~2 minutes more.

Serve with light and bright vegetables and **Shallot Butter** (*p. 165*) enriched with tomatoes and basil.

Mark Marhefka of Abundant Seafood caught this trigger. It has skin like iron, but its flesh is succulent.

Salmon
with Horseradish Crust and Leek Cream

YIELD	TOOLS NEEDED
4 servings	food processor, 2-quart pot

WHEN I WAS GROWING up in the French kitchens, we would use salmon from Scotland or Norway. It was considered a delicacy because it was expensive and hard to get, but it was also well treated. It's not a local fish, but locals and visitors alike love it.

We ran salmon in all sorts of different combinations, but this preparation was, yet again, a sacred cow that had to go so we could move on to other dishes. We still keep it on the lunch menu, however, because our customers told us how much they liked it and wanted it.

It's also a part of the rhythm and balance of our **Cold-Smoked Salmon** (p. 58), with the trimmings from the salmon used to make **Salmon Croquettes** (p. 101), which sell like hotcakes during lunch.

Ingredients

4, 6–8-oz. salmon filets or steaks
2 tablespoons olive oil

HORSERADISH CRUST

2 cups panko
3 tablespoons prepared horseradish
1 cup parsley

LEEK CREAM

2 cups leeks, sliced and washed
1 cup white wine
1 cup **Chicken Stock** (p. 171)
1 cup cream
1 tablespoon butter
½ teaspoon salt
1 teaspoon garlic, minced

Method

Blend all horseradish-crust ingredients together in food processor until well combined.

Leek Cream Method: melt leeks in butter and salt over low heat without browning. Add wine and reduce by ⅔, then add stock and reduce by ½. Add cream, simmer 5 minutes, then add minced garlic.

Press the salmon into the horseradish crust.

Cook over medium heat in olive oil for 4–5 minutes, flip, and cook to mid-rare.

Finish with leek cream.

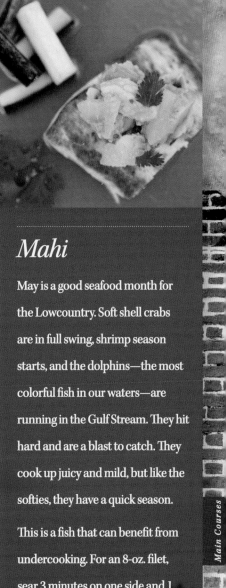

Mahi

May is a good seafood month for the Lowcountry. Soft shell crabs are in full swing, shrimp season starts, and the dolphins—the most colorful fish in our waters—are running in the Gulf Stream. They hit hard and are a blast to catch. They cook up juicy and mild, but like the softies, they have a quick season.

This is a fish that can benefit from undercooking. For an 8-oz. filet, sear 3 minutes on one side and 1 minute on the other. Here, it's featured with **Tomato Coulis** (*p. 168*) and **Avocado-Lime Salad** (*p. 168*).

Main Courses

Simon Pinniger

I never liked swordfish. Tried it one hundred times in one hundred different restaurants, but the taste was always too pungent … until I was invited to S.N.O.B. My host said the fish was always excellent at S.N.O.B., and so it is. Now I look for Chef Lee to put swordfish on the menu, and I order it whenever I can. It is delicious!

Swordfish

W E CAN GET SWORD-FISH locally in Charleston from local boats, typically from Cherry Point Seafood on Wadmalaw Island.

Swordfish are beautiful fish, particularly the "pumpkin" swordfish, the deep orange flesh of which seems even sweeter than its white-fleshed counterparts. And because it's full of fish fat, it grills and sautés beautifully.

This preparation is colorful, crunchy, and it's one of those quintessential S.N.O.B. dishes that doesn't commit you to a big, starchy plate of food.

Method

Take an 8-oz. chunk of swordfish and cut 1½" thick, remove blood line, season lightly and pan sear until barely cooked, ~3 minutes on each side.

Puddle **Basil Pesto** (*p. 166*) on the plate and top with **Tiny Vegetable Vinaigrette** (*p. 177*) and shoestring potatoes.

Barbecue Tuna

YIELD	TOOLS NEEDED
4 servings	heavy frying pan, skillet or grill

THIS IS ANOTHER ONE of those dishes that has some artistic license to it. Even though we do catch tuna in our local waters, you usually have to go to the Gulf Stream to get it. But people love tuna and it's a great fish.

When I got to thinking about it, it occurred to me that tuna is actually a warm-blooded fish. It travels in herds and has red, bloody flesh. So my thought was, "Well, they're kind of like cattle. Why not barbecue them?"

I had to find some way to work in our quintessential South Carolina mustard barbecue sauce, so I dug up this recipe from my friend, Tom Jones, who is an excellent cook. Our mustard 'cue is basically his sauce minus the enormous amount of crushed red pepper he always puts in it. And we make it with molasses, which is fun to do.

The presentation is like a little "drip castle" of oysters on tuna—the country ham butter sauce dripping down into the barbecue with a garnish of green onions and tomato for acidity and color.

But it became another sacred cow. We tried to kill it once, but after a few months, our customers told us we'd lost our minds. Put it back.

It's been one of the quintessential S.N.O.B. dishes and probably one of the few I can say I came up with. Everything else on the menu has always been an interpretation of something else, because it's so rare to have an original idea—it's more about how you execute your technique. But I've never seen this dish anywhere else, and even though I made it kind of goofy, people love it. Barbecued tuna: a goofy dish that actually works.

Ingredients

1 batch **Mustard BBQ Sauce** *(P. 163)*

1 batch **Country Ham Green Onion Butter Sauce** *(P. 164)*

4, 8-oz. portions of tuna loin

olive oil

24 oysters, shucked

2 cups cornmeal

2 cups cooking oil

Method

Roll oyster meat in cornmeal.

Fry in ~1"oil and heat until hot: 350°.

Fry oysters ~40 seconds. Remove and drain on paper towel. Keep warm.

Lightly brush tuna with olive oil and sauté or grill until medium-rare.

Glaze tuna with mustard BBQ sauce, then remove from heat immediately.

To assemble: Zig zag the mustard BBQ sauce onto the plate. Stack oysters on tuna and dribble with butter sauce.

Jack and Theresa Lubbers

We have been going to S.N.O.B. for many years and have favorite seats at the chef's table, where we can watch the kitchen workers in action and meet members of the staff and other diners. We often find ourselves offering suggestions to first-time visitors, including our favorites such as the swordfish, scallops, barbecue tuna, shrimp and grits, pear salad, and lamb chops.

Shrimp and Grits

WE DIDN'T START OFF serving shrimp and grits. At first we were doing a deconstructed Frogmore stew, then we took away the potatoes to keep it light, doing a quick sauté of the sausage and peppers and shrimp and corn with a little bit of Cajun spice and shrimp stock, finishing it with a touch of butter and green onions.

That quickly grew into shrimp and grits, but we still kept that mind-set of sautéing the shrimp with sausage and tomatoes and green onions.

In 1994 we won an award from *GQ* magazine for it: the Golden Dish Award for shrimp and grits, which was kind of bittersweet because I'd rather have won an award for doing the Palmetto Pigeon. But when people come to Charleston, they want something that they see as representing Charleston. For us, that means doing our best to present a shrimp and grits dish that has quality and integrity and reflects our region.

The version we use today is one that we've had for ten years or more. We use the **Kielbasa Sausage** (p. 69) that we make in-house with local shrimp and grits that we get from the Geechie Boy Mill out on Edisto Island.

It's a gussied-up version of the shrimp and grits I had as a kid. You'd think it was something that only visitors ordered, but that's not the case. Locals and visitors enjoy it alike.

NOTE: *This is a sauté; a quick jump into a hot pan. You want to sear the shrimp, not burn the spice, release the tomatoes, and add just enough stock to create a pan sauce tightened with the butter without overcooking the shrimp. Now, do it correctly in under 15 minutes, 22,000 times a year while cooking five other dishes in your station. That's part of what it takes to be a Cuisine Commando.*

Ingredients

1 recipe creamy **Grits** (p. 79)

20 shrimp, peeled and deveined

4 oz. country ham, julienned

4 oz. **Kielbasa Sausage** (p. 69)

1 cup fresh tomato, peeled, seeded, and medium-diced

1 cup green onion

1 teaspoon garlic, minced

2 teaspoons Cajun spice

2–3 oz. **Shrimp Stock** (p. 172)

2 tablespoons butter

Method

Brown the ham and sausage with 1 tablespoon butter.

Add the shrimp, garlic, Cajun spice, and sauté without burning the spice: ~2 minutes.

Add the tomatoes and green onion, continuing to sauté until the tomato renders some juice.

Moisten with the shrimp stock and bring to a bubble (not a boil), and finish with butter.

Main Courses

Dianne Boersman

Anne brought me here for the first time after I retired, and eating lunch with her at Slightly North of Broad every Friday for the past several years has become our tradition. For my birthday one year, we all decided to have steak. Afterward, they remembered how much we loved chocolate mousse and brought one out—a single chocolate mousse with four spoons in it. It was wonderful!

Linda Disher

I've been coming here to S.N.O.B. with Mrs. Moskowitz every Friday ever since I retired, and I'm slowly but surely learning to enjoy fish. Growing up in Ohio, I was used to beans, beef, and chicken, but the fish here is just delicious.

Kay Dydek

Mrs. Moskowitz and I were in a book club together and she kept insisting that I come to Slightly North of Broad with her once I retired. It wasn't a week after my last day at work that she brought me in for her weekly Friday lunch. The first dish I had was the flounder, and it was incredible—perfectly done and moist. I've been coming back with her every Friday since then for more than seven years.

Anne-Leone Moskowitz

I have been coming to Slightly North of Broad since 1999; every Tuesday until Peter (Pierce, general manager) switched his schedule, so I switched mine so that I wouldn't miss him. Peter really is one-of-a-kind. He and the staff here remember everything—that I love the French bread, what I can and can't have—all those little things so that every time I eat here, it's a treat.

Soft Shell Crab

YIELD	TOOLS NEEDED
4 servings	kitchen scissors, frying pan

SOFT SHELL CRABS ARE one of the harbingers of summer in Charleston, and when it comes in, it literally dominates the menu, outselling everything else 4-to-1. There's big competition between chefs every year to see who can get them on their menu first, even though it's just a matter of days before everyone does.

It's hard to tell when the season will officially start, since the conditions have to be just right for the crab to molt. Typically, it's right around when the tidal water reaches 70 degrees and coincides with a full moon. And if we're lucky, we'll get a brief second season in late September when the water drops back to 70 degrees for two or three weeks.

We've prepared soft shell crab several different ways over the years, grilling them, frying them, sautéing them. And of course, we run them as a sandwich at lunch. It's always great to see 'em come—and great to see 'em go. Soft shell crab is fine eating, however you choose to prepare it.

Ingredients

4 fresh soft shell crabs with apron, lungs, eyes, and mouth removed with scissors

¼ pound clarified butter

1½ cups gluten-free **Calabash Crumbs** (*p. 123*)

1 teaspoon salt

2 oz. white wine

2 tablespoons minced spring onion bulb or shallot

1 tablespoon capers, rinsed

2 lemons: 1 juiced and 1 quartered

½ cup parsley, medium-diced

½ pound butter

asparagus, **Blanched** (*p. 72*)

pea tendrils

Method

Dust cleaned crab in flour and fry in clarified butter until crispy brown.

Remove crabs from pan, pour off excess clarified butter, add shallots, and deglaze pan with wine.

Add capers, and swirl in whole butter, lemon juice, and parsley.

Toss the asparagus and pea shoots in **Lemon Shallot Dressing** (*p. 177*) and serve alongside the buttery crabs.

Jumbo Lump Crab Cakes with Corn Sauce

YIELD	TOOLS NEEDED
2-4 servings	skillet

USUALLY, WHEN PEOPLE ASK me what to serve with a main course meat, I say, "Well, what does the critter eat? Maybe we can pair that up with the dish." Crabs don't eat corn, but there's something about corn that goes so well with crab. So we'd pair this with a beautiful **Corn Sauce** (p. 78) and barrels of okra, topping it all with our secret weapon: **Pepper Relish** (p. 182).

The jumbo lump crab cakes originally replaced our deviled crab cakes, which we ran until it finally became another one of those sacred cows. We had to kill it—get it off the menu so we could run other dishes that were exciting and relevant.

Ingredients

1 pound jumbo lump crab meat

1 egg, beaten

¼ teaspoon nutmeg, ground

½ teaspoon salt

½ teaspoon white pepper, ground

¼ cup panko

¼ cup cream

¼ cup vegetable oil

Method

Gently toss ingredients together.

Refrigerate 1 hour before forming into cakes.

Heat oil and pan fry cakes ~4 minutes on each side.

Deviled Crab Cakes in the Shell

All of South Carolina—and Charleston in particular—has incredible local crabs, though we're hard-pressed to find any local crab production houses nearby. When we had a crab picker like Eddie Gordon of McClellanville Crab Company around, we had the great privilege of using his crabmeat for all our crab needs.

Serving crab in the shell is old school, and it looks great. Catch and pick your own crabs to truly enjoy the flavors of the Lowcountry.

Tools needed: baking sheet or pan

Yield: 2–4 servings

Ingredients:

1 pound crab meat, picked clean of shells

½ cup red bell pepper, small-diced

½ cup small red onion, small-diced

½ cup parsley, medium-diced

2 lemons, juiced

1 teaspoon Tabasco

¾ teaspoon Worcestershire

1 teaspoon pepper

½ teaspoon salt

1 tablespoon yellow mustard

1 egg, lightly beaten

2 tablespoons mayonnaise

4 crab shells

4 teaspoons butter

½–¾ cup **Calabash Crumbs** (p. 123) or panko

Method:

- Preheat oven to 375°.
- Mix thoroughly all ingredients except crab shells, butter, and crumbs/panko.
- Generously fill crab shells with mixture and dot each with butter and crumbs.
- Bake until hot, ~20 minutes.

Scallops

PART OF THE INTEGRITY that we maintain as S.N.O.B. is looking for product that's not treated with chemicals, which is difficult when it comes to seafood like scallops and shrimp, since they've historically been treated with sodium tripolyphosphate and sodium bisulfate. These chemicals keep the flesh white while also swelling it up with water and making it feel slippery. It keeps the protein from spoiling, but it does nothing to improve the quality of the natural product.

The challenge was finding scallops that hadn't been treated with chemicals at all and that were minimally processed. We found two characters out of Myrtle Beach that fit the bill: Mark and Mark. They were restaurateurs who sold their business in New Bedford and moved down south only to get bored and open a new business, Northern Seafood Express.

> **Method for Searing Scallops:**
> - Season scallops on all sides with salt and pepper.
> - Sear in 1 tablespoon olive oil over medium heat for 30 seconds on each side until brown.

Since they both had good friends who are also scallopers, they'd get their buddies to bring them the top of the boat: last one on, first one off. They'd send those scallops down from Boston by plane, and they were of gorgeous quality every time. They had great caramelization, browning up in the pan beautifully, with all the quality, integrity, and consistency that is the hallmark of Slightly North of Broad.

My old friend and legendary Pawley's Island chef Louis Osteen turned us on to them and shortly after we started buying from them Bob Waggoner and Michelle at Charleston Grille started using them, too. Now, several years later, they have a burgeoning business in Charleston and they're still getting us beautiful scallops.

"If you're worried about whether the scallops are cooked through, undercooked scallops are better than overcooked. Overcooked scallops are terrible, so you want to keep them a nice mid-rare."

—cookbook photographer

Seared Scallops in Vegetable Nest with Scallop Cream

YIELD	TOOLS NEEDED
4 servings	skillet

Ingredients

16 quality scallops

1 cup each, julienned:

   red onion

   snow pea pods

   red bell pepper

   carrots

   zucchini squash

1 tablespoon butter

salt

Method

Blanch all vegetables except for zucchini, then warm all vegetables, including zucchini, in butter and salt to taste.

Make a nest out of vegetables and place "eggs"—seared **Scallops** (*p. 140*)—in the nest, surrounded by a thin moat of **Scallop Cream** (*p. 141*).

Scallop Cream

When we clean our shucked scallops, there is a tough connecting membrane (called the "feet"), which we remove and save to make our scallop cream.

Tools needed:

2-quart pot

Yield: 5 cups

Ingredients:

2 tablespoons butter

1 pound scallop feet or pieces

1 cup sliced shallots

¼ teaspoon salt

1 cup white wine

2 cups cream

Method:

- Cook the scallops, shallots, butter, and salt in the pot over medium heat until caramelization begins—~20 minutes—stirring constantly as the mixture becomes more caramelized. Don't scorch it!

- Deglaze with white wine and reduce until sticky.

- Add cream and bring to a simmer, then cover pot and remove from heat.

- Allow to rest for 30 minutes, then strain through a *chinoise*, discarding solids.

D U C K

WHEN I WAS GROWING up, duck was always one of my favorite dishes. My mom would cook it for us maybe once every two months because she had to order it from the butcher shop and wait for them to bring it in. But when she did, we'd have a whole roast duck that was crazy good.

In the early days at S.N.O.B., we'd serve you half a duck, with the breast cooked the moment you order it to the temperature you wanted, getting the skin all brown and crispy, and serving it along with the thigh and leg cooked **Confit** (*p. 145*). We'd pair that with a **Yellow Squash Casserole** (*p. 71*) with green beans and a sauce we made with passion fruit purée and reduced duck stock.

Getting in that whole duck fits right into our rhythm of *mise en place*. We create the confit from the legs and thighs and necks and gizzards, and the liver goes right into **Patés** (*p. 61*) and **Mousses** (*p. 66*). The brown duck carcasses are chopped up and used to make **Stock** (*p. 170*), and the fat can be cross-utilized in dozens of recipes.

Duck has always served a purpose on the S.N.O.B. menu. It gives people choices. It's rich and flavorful and it's not something you often cook at home.

Duck Breast

YIELD	TOOLS NEEDED
1 serving	cast iron skillet

Method

Trim an 8–10 oz. breast of silver skin and extra skin on the edges.

Season the breast liberally with salt and pepper
and a touch of garam masala.

Cook in skillet, skin-side down over medium low
heat for 15 minutes, rendering the fat from the
skin and developing a crispy brown coat.

Flip breast over and continue another 3 minutes
or until mid-rare to medium.

Remove from the pan and allow to rest at least 5 minutes.

When the juices have settled and the meat is plump and satisfied,
lay it skin-side down and give it 5 confident slices on a bias.

Scoop the sliced breast onto the flat of your blade and flip the
meat attractively onto the plate: rosy, tender, and inviting.

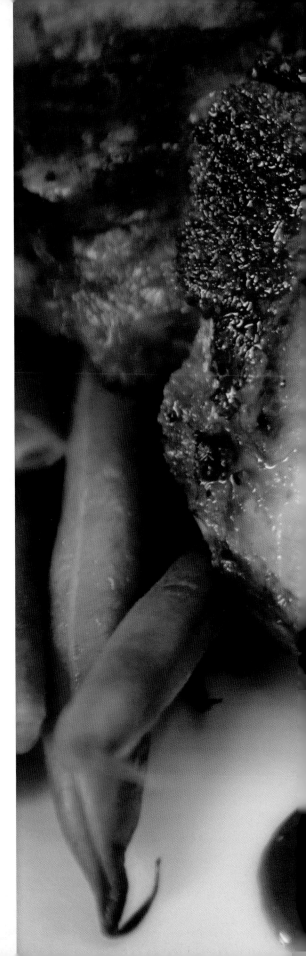

Duck Confit

Confit is another one of those French terms. It literally means "to preserve." You can cook a vegetable confit or a duck leg. Or a fish or a chicken or a platypus; it doesn't matter.

Confit was one of the original ways to preserve meat in northern Europe. Before refrigerators, most people had root cellars. So they'd cook the meat in its fat and then let it cool that way so it was sealed all around. With no air getting to it and the root cellar staying around 50 to 45 degrees or cooler, that meat could last for months. But once you disturbed the meat and let oxygen get in there, you needed to use it.

Brining or salting the meat before it goes in the fat makes it scrumptious, and it's a great tool for using things up.

This is a quick confit without curing. We use up our duck legs in a matter of days and have no need to preserve the legs longer with salt.

Method:

- Remove the thick leg bone from 2 duck leg quarters.
- Place in 2-quart pot with:
  - 1 head garlic cut in ½
  - 1 teaspoon thyme, medium-diced
  - 1 teaspoon whole cloves
  - 1 teaspoon whole black peppercorns
  - 1 teaspoon salt

  Cover with 4 cups rendered duck fat.

  Cook over low heat or bake in 300° oven for ~2 hours or until a thin blade can penetrate the thigh with no resistance.

  Remove garlic and refrigerate in the fat.

P O R K

PORK IS ANOTHER ONE of those la-
bors of love at S.N.O.B. We'll get in whole
pork loins that need to be broken down
or half pigs that take a lot of time to bone
out. With the whole pigs, we'll also get that
thick, rich, creamy, beautiful fatback and
use that in different preparations. Then
there's the neck and legs and shanks
and some peripheral bony meat that
we'll either use to make our **Patés**
(*p. 64*) and **Sausages** (*p. 69*), or we'll
braise it, pull it, and make it into
some kind of barbecue.

We'll make hams out of the bigger muscles and tasso out of some of the belly.
And of course, we'll run pork belly.

Pork is definitely a rhythm we ride at the restaurant, and we never stray far from it. It plays
a big role on our menu, and it's satisfying to see a
cured and well-prepared sliced pork with a nice gravy
and bright green vegetables going out.

Pork Chop

CHESHIRE FARMS UP IN North Carolina makes a nice pork chop that they used to sell exclusively to Japan and only recently opened up to the Southeast. The pigs are bred to have fat in their meat, which is what makes it prime. It gives their pork chops this great tenderness and richness, and they do it well consistently.

We take the chops and brine them for two hours, then we **Cold Smoke** (*p. 59*) them for two more hours and grill them. We pair that with confit potatoes and melted cabbage, a nice little sauce, and some relish.

Method

Brine (method below) one 10–12 oz. pork chop 1–2 hours.

Pat dry and **Cold Smoke** (*p. 59*) for an hour or more.

Lightly oil, season the chop, and grill 8–10 minutes on one side, and 5–8 minutes on the other.

Serve with **Sorghum Glaze** (recipe below).

Sorghum Glaze

Yield: 2 cups

Tools needed: 2-quart pot

Ingredients:

1 cup sorghum
1 cup whole-grain mustard
½ cup apple cider vinegar

Method:

- Combine and simmer for 5 minutes.

Brining Method

Ingredients:

2 cups salt
2 cups sugar
½ gallon water
¼ cup pickling spice

Method:

- Bring to boil and add ½ gallon ice. Let it melt and strain it off.

Main Courses

BEEF

BEEF TENDERLOIN HAS ALWAYS been a big seller on our menu, but it's fun to play around with all the varietal cuts. We ran hangar, flank, and flatiron steak for the longest time, and of course we had New York strip and ribeyes from time to time.

When Stevenson Place Farms in Greenwood, South Carolina, delivered practically a whole cow to us twice a month, we'd use the bones for beef stock, the tongue and brisket for corned beef, and we'd make wonderful braises like **Beef Stew with Olives** (*p. 102*). We'd prepare **Carpaccio** (*p. 109*) from the eye of the round, and every now and then, we'd have enough loins to run a special. We'd do everything we could to use it all up.

That went on for about twelve years, until the farm stopped selling to restaurants, but it was a great program while it lasted. It was a lot of effort on their part, and it was a big undertaking for us, as well. There were times when we'd end up with 150 pounds of bones and no kettles—so we'd have to use stock pots, filling up every burner and running them overnight. I pity the fool that had to do the prep the next day, straining off those giant pots of stock, reducing them, and starting them all up again.

Beef Tenderloin
with Deviled Crab Cake, Béarnaise, and Green Peppercorn Sauce

YIELD	TOOLS NEEDED
1 serving	grill or skillet

ONE OF THOSE BEEF dishes that we rode hard for fifteen years or more was a beef tenderloin with **Deviled Crab Cake** (*p. 139*) topped with **Béarnaise Sauce** (*p. 165*) and a **Green Peppercorn Reduction** (*p. 175*). It's an excellent dish that people enjoy and one that I had absolutely no creative input on. Béarnaise sauce was figured out long before I made it (although I am fond of my version). Green peppercorn sauce is about as classic as you get, and beef tenderloin is a very popular dish.

It didn't change much over the years. We went to a jumbo lump crab cake instead of a deviled crab cake, but we always served it simply, with a grilled tomato with basil. It was so popular that we finally had to kill the sacred cow to make room for new dishes.

Ingredients

1, 8-oz. beef tenderloin, center-cut
1, 3-oz. **Deviled Crab Cake** (*p. 139*)
1 oz. **Green Peppercorn Sauce** (*p. 165*)
1 oz. **Béarnaise Sauce** (*p. 175*)
1 teaspoon salt
1 teaspoon pepper
1 tablespoon olive oil

Method

Lightly oil and then liberally season beef filet with salt and pepper.

Grill or pan roast beef to internal temperature of 105°–110° for medium-rare, remove from heat, and allow to rest 5 minutes.

At the same time, pan-fry the deviled crab cake until cooked through.

Serve on a hot plate, spooning green peppercorn sauce over the beef, placing the crab cake on top, and adding a stripe of béarnaise across the crab.

CHICKEN

CHICKEN HAS AN INTERESTING role in the kitchen. We do it so many different ways, and it has a constant presence as a stock on the back burner. It's part of our foundation, serving it at lunch and working its way into dishes as stock, but it's never found a home on the nighttime menu, where it's always lost the competition to duck and quail. It plays a big role in our Lunch Express, however, from Southern fried chicken on Saturday to chicken and dumplings.

Chicken Stock (*P. 171*) is the lifeblood of our kitchen. It's ubiquitous. We have it on the stove probably four or five days out of the week, where it serves as one of the foundations on which we build our rhythm of *mise en place*. It's one of those things that separated Slightly North of Broad in the beginning and even today. It's part of our respect for the animal and using it all up.

At the same time, when you think about chicken, you have to think about which came first. We support many of our local chicken egg producers, starting with Celeste Albers at the Green Grocer and then buying from Annie Filion at Keegan-Filion Farms. We like to use them in things like the **Crème Brûlée** (*P. 191*) and the **Key Lime Pie** (*P. 188*) because they give the dishes this intense yellow color that comes from all the greens the chickens eat. It's a wonderful thing.

*Annie Filion's chicken breast with **Okra Pilaf** (P. 93) and **Big G's Dried White Limas** (P. 95). We brine the chicken for several hours, then brown it in the pan and roast it for 20 minutes at 400 degrees.*

Dinner at Home

The quintessential meal for my wife and me is mustard greens and some roast chicken with pepper relish. Nothing suits me better.

We bake a whole chicken in our Romertopf clay cooker, which cooks it really tender and juicy. Before it's over, we throw in a handful of mirepoix and garlic, just in time for them to finish at the same time as the chicken.

While that's going on, we cook up a big **Rutabaga** (*p. 88*) the same way my dad used to do it, cook down some **Rice** (*p. 81*) and butterbeans, whip up a **Field Pea Ragout** (*p. 90*), and serve it all with **Pepper Relish** (*p. 182*).

It just doesn't get much better than that.

For chefs, the challenge is how to make these meals (that may take three hours at home) and bring them to the plate in 15 or 20 minutes. You have to use your craft to figure that out.

Thanksgiving Turkey

Y
ou can't mention poultry and you can't think local without thinking of Annie Filion and her turkeys. Annie's farm, Keegan-Filion Farms, is located about an hour southwest of Charleston in Walterboro, and we've been serving her turkeys for Thanksgiving since about 2006.

It's such a pleasure to be able to go out and watch her turkeys growing. It's one of the rhythms we have with the season, the rhythm of Thanksgiving and the rhythm of the turkeys.

Every November, we get 25 or more large birds at one time, and we have to bone out each one; brine and roast the legs, breasts, and thighs; make turkey **Stock** (*p. 170*) and gravy; and have them all ready for Thanksgiving dinner. It's a week-long commitment, but it's very rewarding; her turkeys just taste better.

RABBIT

ABOUT ONCE A WEEK, for a good long while, we ran a dish with rabbit from Dean Goforth of Dean's Rabbits up in Fountain Inn, South Carolina.

The farm-raised rabbits are very tender, but there's not a whole lot of meat on them. Since they came with their kidneys and livers, we'd take the livers to make **Paté** (*p. 63*) and bone out the whole rabbit. The forelegs would go into **Confit** (*p. 145*) or a **Rillette** (*p. 62*), and the haunch, which has the most meat, would either be stuffed and roasted or cooked confit, braised, and made into a great stew.

It was very appealing to say, "braised rabbit haunch with spring vegetables and pearl onions and mushrooms." Serve with gnocchi, and you're done.

Yeah that's a big SLAB o' Foie gras
In the middle of the plate.
NO, it's not in the recipe.

Braised
Rabbit Haunch

YIELD	TOOLS NEEDED
4 servings	skillet, casserole dish or Dutch oven with lid

This recipe can also be made with chicken or duck leg quarters instead of rabbit.

Ingredients

4 rabbit haunches

salt

pepper

1 cup flour or rice flour (gluten-free)

¼ cup olive oil

½ cup mirepoix

2 fennel stalks, small-diced

1 bay leaf

1 teaspoon fresh thyme

1 teaspoon fresh tarragon

Method

Prepare the haunch by loosening the meat from the thighbone and inverting the meat down over the small drumstick, leaving the thighbone exposed as a handle. Or simply remove the thighbone and retain the natural shape of the haunch.

Lightly season the haunch with salt and pepper, then dredge in flour or rice flour and brown in hot olive oil over medium heat.

To braise, sweat *mirepoix* and fennel stalks in olive oil with a touch of salt. When vegetables are tender, sprinkle in a little flour and stir to incorporate.

Add the haunch, herbs, and just enough chicken stock to cover meat ½ way up. The goal here is to gently braise, not boil, the meat and create a rich, concentrated braising liquid.

Cook covered at 325° for 1½ hours or until meat is tender, not blasted and "falling off the bone."

Plate the meat, strain the jus back over it, and garnish with fresh, colorful vegetables—or place on grits enriched with lemon zest and lemon juice.

yeah, those are turne' vegetables

Main Courses

Roast Rabbit (or Chicken) Roulade

Tools needed: skillet, butcher's twine

Yield: 2 servings

Ingredients:

1 rabbit

4 oz. **Chicken Mousse** (*p. 67*) enriched with rabbit trimmings

1 batch **Madeira Sauce** (*p. 175*)

Method:

- Heat oven to 350°.
- Butcher the bunny, retaining the forelegs to make **Rillette** (*p. 62*), the haunch for a braise, the bones for **Stock** (*p. 170*), and the liver for **Paté** (*p. 63*).
- Remove the two loins and thin breast meat intact and roll up with rabbit-enriched Chicken Mousse (*p. 67*).
- Tie roulades loosely with butcher's twine evenly in three places.
- Brown evenly on all sides in skillet, then finish in oven, baking until internal temperature is 160°. Allow to rest 10 minutes before serving.
- Just before serving, remove twine and slice, finishing with **Madeira Sauce** (*p. 175*).
- Serve with sautéed bok choy and sprigs of tarragon.

Main Courses

L A M B

LAMB, LIKE DUCK, IS another one of those meals that goes back to my childhood. We probably had leg of lamb every month, with Mom roasting the leg whole and cooking it well done. It was wonderful.

For Dad's part, he would make this mint *gastrique* to go on the lamb instead of mint jelly. It was a recipe that I'm sure he picked up in Chicago. There was sugar and vinegar and lots of fresh mint chopped in at the last second. Take that, splash it over your leg of lamb with the pan juices, and it was pretty darn good.

Later, when I went to Chicago and worked at Les Nomades with Jovan, we would do the *gigot d'agneau* quite often. But when I came down to Charleston, very few restaurants were offering it. So we started doing roast leg of lamb, offering it with our version of **Dad's Mint Vinegar** (*p. 163*) and served with **Scalloped Sweet Potatoes with Horseradish Cream** (*p. 88*)

Rack of Lamb

YIELD

1 rack of lamb

TOOLS NEEDED

heavy skillet

Ingredients

1, 12–14 oz.
rack of lamb

1 teaspoon salt

1 teaspoon pepper

2 tablespoons
canola oil

2 oz. **Rosemary Red
Wine Sauce** (*P. 175*)

1, 4-oz. serving of
**Scalloped Sweet
Potatoes with
Horseradish
Cream** (*P. 88*)

Method

Preheat oven to 400°.

Season rack liberally with
salt and pepper, and
let rack acclimate to
room temperature.

Heat skillet with canola
oil and get it hot.

Sear the rack meat-side
down for 2 minutes, then
flip over and roast in the
oven for 10 minutes or
until internal temperature
is 105° for medium-rare.

Allow rack to rest at least 10
minutes before slicing.

Finish with rosemary red
wine sauce and serve with
scalloped sweet potatoes
with horseradish cream.

Roast Leg of Lamb with Dad's Mint Vinegar

Method:

- Clean sliver skin and pockets of fat from 1, 5-6 pound boneless leg of lamb, avoiding piercing the outer skin.

- Rub the inside with garlic, salt, pepper, and sprinkle with 1 cup diced mint, reserving half the rub for later.

- Tie gently with butcher's twine and let rest, refrigerated, overnight.

- When ready to roast, season the outside with rub and acclimate leg to room temperature: ~30 minutes.

- Roast in 375° oven, turning twice, until internal temperature reaches a medium 130°, ~1 hour. Rest 15 minutes before carving.

Serve with **Green Farro** (*p. 81*) and roasted fennel bulbs.

SAUCES

SAUCES ARE SOME OF my favorite things to do. People ask me all the time what I like to cook, and I say that I gravitate toward seasonal fish and vegetables, poultry and sauces. When you're a saucier, like Matthew Niessner of Hall's Chophouse, you're at the top of the food chain, reaping the benefit of all the *mise en place* in the kitchen. At the same time, you're using up a lot of those extra parts, putting your hands up into guts, digging around blood vessels, feeling muscles, and goozling bones. It's a very visceral experience and very sensual—and good for the immune system, too, in my opinion.

Dad's Mint Vinegar

Tools needed: 2-quart nonreactive pot

Yield: 1 cup

Ingredients:

¼ cup red onion minced

1 cup red wine vinegar

½ cup water

¼ cup sugar

1 cup mint, medium-diced

Method:

- Bring all ingredients to a boil, then chill.

Mustard BBQ Sauce

Tools needed: 2-quart nonreactive pot, *chinoise*

Yield: 1 quart

Ingredients:

2 cups white vinegar

2 cups yellow mustard

¾ cup ketchup

½ cup sweet molasses

½ cup dark honey

1 cup water

1 tablespoon Worcestershire

1 teaspoon Tabasco

2 teaspoons crushed red pepper

Method:

- Combine all ingredients in pot.
- Bring to a simmer, stirring often, and cook for 15 minutes to get the rawness of the vinegar off and to thicken.
- Strain through a *chinoise*.

White Wine Cream Sauce

This is great with the **Grouper Terrine** (*p. 68*) or poached trout, salmon, or halibut.

Tools needed: nonreactive skillet, *chinoise*

Yield: 2 cups

Ingredients:

1 cup shallots, fine-diced

1 cup white of leek, fine-diced

1 cup parsley stems, fine-diced

1 cup white mushroom, small-sliced

2 fresh bay leaves

1 tablespoon fresh thyme

3 cups white wine

3 cups **Fish Stock** (*p. 172*)

2 cups cream

2 tablespoons butter

Method:

- Sweat the vegetables with 2 tablespoons butter without browning.
- Add white wine, bay leaves, and thyme, and reduce until almost dry.
- Add fish stock and reduce by two-thirds, then add cream and simmer over low heat 5 minutes.

Black Jack BBQ Sauce

Tools needed: 2-quart nonreactive pot

Yield: 2 cups

Ingredients:

1 cup black coffee

½ cup Worcestershire

1 cup ketchup

½ cup apple cider vinegar

½ cup light brown sugar

2 teaspoons salt

1 cup yellow onion, small-diced

1 teaspoon crushed red pepper flakes

Method:

- Combine all ingredients in pot and simmer, cooking until sticky (~15 minutes), then chill.

Country Ham Green Onion Butter Sauce

Tools needed: skillet

Yield: 1 cup

Ingredients:

4 oz. country ham, julienned

8 oz. **Fish Stock** (*p. 172*)

½ cup green onion, medium-diced

6 oz. butter

Method:

- Cook ham in stock and reduce by ⅔.
- Whisk in butter, add green onions, and set aside.

Béarnaise

Matthew Niessner is the only chef I've met who makes béarnaise like I do. We make it with a tarragon reduction that we've made every night for close to two decades. It's an in-your-face kind of béarnaise, and that tarragon reduction keeps forever in the cooler.

Tools needed: heavy bowl, whisk

Yield: 1 cup

Ingredients:

4 egg yolks

2 tablespoons water

⅛ teaspoon salt

½ teaspoon lemon juice

1 dash Tabasco

2 tablespoons **Tarragon Reduction** (*p. 167*)

6 oz. whole butter, room temperature

Method:

- Whip the yolks, water, and salt together in bowl and cook over low heat, whisking vigorously and working the edges until the mixture is thickening, fluffy, and hot. Avoid scrambling the yolks.

- Whisk in the lemon juice, Tabasco, tarragon reduction, and continue to whisk in the butter, ⅓ at a time, over the heat. Whisk until all butter is incorporated and the béarnaise has the consistency of mayonnaise. The whole process should take ~10 minutes and will hold in a warm spot for 3–4 hours, maximum.

- Add fish stock and reduce by two-thirds, then add cream and simmer over low heat 5 minutes.

Shallot Butter Sauce

This basic fish butter can be used as a vehicle for enhancing all kinds of flavorful combinations such as chives, lemon and dill, capers and Dijon mustard, finely diced tomatoes and basil, etc.

Tools needed: nonreactive skillet

Yield: 1 cup

Ingredients:

1 cup shallots, fine-diced

1 cup champagne vinegar

2 cups **Fish Stock** (*p. 172*)

¼ pound, plus 1 tablespoon butter

pinch of salt

Method:

- Sweat the shallots in 1 tablespoon butter without browning.

- Add vinegar and reduce until almost dry, then add fish stock and reduce by two-thirds.

- Whisk in butter and season with salt.

Shiitake Mushroom Butter Sauce

Tools needed: skillet, whisk

Yield: 4 servings

Ingredients:

4 cups shiitake mushrooms, sliced

½ cup shallots, sliced

¼ teaspoon salt

2 cups **Fish Stock** (*p. 172*)

6 oz. plus 1 tablespoon butter

1 tablespoon fresh lemon juice

Method:

- Sweat mushrooms, salt, and 1 tablespoon butter.

- When soft, add stock and reduce to ⅓, then whisk in 6 oz. butter.

- Remove from heat and add lemon juice.

Basil Pesto

My daughter Meghan is allergic to pine nuts, so we make our basil pesto with almonds. The basil is blanched, which gives it a bright green color. It looks incredible on the plate.

Tools needed: blender, kitchen towel

Yield: 1½ cups

Ingredients:

4 oz. basil, picked, **Blanched** (*p. 72*), squeezed, and dried

¼ cup grated Parmigiano-Reggiano

¼ cup sliced almonds

2 teaspoons garlic, minced

½–¾ cup olive oil

Method:

· Blanch basil, then dry by rolling leaves up in a towel and squeezing.

· Rough chop the basil, then put all ingredients in blender and purée.

Plum Glaze

At one point, one of our farmers started bringing in big baskets filled with tiny plums, which were excellent but hard to work with. So we put them in a pot with sugar and vinegar and jalapeños, cooked them down, mushed them up, and strained them off. The result was this beautiful, dramatic, ruby-red glaze with a fruity, piquant flavor that lends itself to crispy, fatty meats such as squab, duck, turkey, pork chop, etc.

Tools needed: 2-gallon pot, *chinoise*

Yield: 6 cups

Ingredients:

3 pounds whole plums

2 cups sugar

1 cup apple cider vinegar

1 cup water

¼ cup fresh ginger, peeled and diced

¼ teaspoon salt

Method:

- Put all ingredients in a 2-gallon pot and bring to a boil, then cover and turn heat down to low. Cook 15 minutes.
- Mash fruit with a whip to release pits, then purée the flesh.
- Pass through a medium *chinoise* and discard pits and bits of skin.

Tomato Jalapeño Cilantro Salsa

Another excuse for me to use cilantro, this all-purpose salsa is good as is or with fish, chicken, and of course, tacos!

Tools needed: mixing bowl

Yield: 4 cups

Ingredients:

¼ cup balsamic vinegar

2 teaspoons salt

2 teaspoons garlic, mashed

2 tablespoons jalapeño, diced with seeds

4 cups tomatoes, peeled, seeded, and fine-diced

¼ cup fresh cilantro, medium-diced

3 tablespoons olive oil

Method:

- Mix the vinegar with the salt and garlic. Let macerate for 5 minutes, then add the jalapeño, tomatoes, cilantro, and olive oil.

Tarragon Reduction

We use this for our béarnaise, but it can be added to anything that needs a tart tarragon bump, like a brown veal mushroom reduction, a fricassee of chicken, or a shellfish *veloute*. The reduction keeps forever when refrigerated.

Tools needed: nonreactive skillet

Yield: 1 cup

Ingredients:

1 cup red onion, fine-diced

½ cup dry tarragon

2 cups red wine vinegar

Method:

- In the skillet, combine all ingredients and reduce to a slush.

Avocado-Lime Salad

Bright and light, the lime supreme makes it special.

Tools needed: stainless steel bowl

Yield: 2 cups

Ingredients:

3 Haas avocados, large-diced

3 limes, supreme (segments without pith, membrane, or seed), reserve 4 tablespoons juice

½ teaspoon garlic, minced

1 teaspoon salt

1 tablespoon cilantro, medium-diced

Method:

- Peel and supreme the lime, retaining the juice.
- Combine lime and juice with garlic and salt in bowl, then add avocado and cilantro. Toss gently.

Tomato Coulis

In-season, we always have too many tomatoes—to the point where we have to assign tomato-patrol duty to harvest the overripe ones. This is a great way to use up overripe tomatoes.

Tools needed: a pot with lid, large-hole *chinoise*, food processor, ladle

Yield: 10 cups

Ingredients:

4 cups onion, sliced

½ cup olive oil

1 teaspoon salt

1 tablespoon brown sugar

1 tablespoon garlic, minced

1 gallon tomatoes, quartered

2 tablespoons tomato paste

Method:

- Place onions, olive oil, salt, and brown sugar in a pot. Add tomatoes and tomato paste on top, cover, and cook over medium-high heat until boiling.
- Turn heat down and simmer for 30 minutes.
- Pass through large-hole *chinoise*, then purée remaining pulp in food processor. Mix puréed pulp back into the jus and mix.
- Strain once more through *chinoise*, pushing through with ladle.
- Serve with fish, with Avocado Lime Salad and topped with cilantro.

Passion Fruit Coulis

A dessert sauce that can be varied with any number of fresh berry purées, such as raspberry or blackberry.

Tools needed: 1-quart pot

Yield: 1 cup

Ingredients:

½ cup sugar

¼ cup water

½ cup passion fruit purée (or juice)

1⅓ teaspoon cornstarch

1 tablespoon water

Method:

- Mix cornstarch in water and set aside.
- Boil sugar and ¼ cup water, add passion fruit, and bring back up to boil.
- Add cornstarch slurry and cook until thickened.

Mel Davidson

 When I walked into the S.N.O.B. kitchen on my first day, a kinda crazy-looking man cleaning shrimp in the corner made eye contact with me. He had a sweet smile, dark-rimmed glasses, and curls of unruly hair peeking out from under a chili pepper ball cap. I wandered over to introduce myself, and he said, "Hi, I'm Frank Lee." My jaw dropped in awe to meet such a humble force. Just like that, my love and affection for the brilliance of Frank Lee began—the only one I'll ever call "mi hefe," my Chef.

Jason Capps

chef/owner, Bella Sera, Canonsburg, PA

 I remember the day I was interviewed and hired by Chef Frank Lee. I was so excited! S.N.O.B. had just opened a year or so prior and was packed every day for lunch and dinner. I asked Chef what I needed to bring with me to work, assuming he would say, "Knives, nonslip shoes, garde-manger kit, etc. . . ." Instead he casually replied, "Don't bring anything but your socks." I had no idea what that meant! What I quickly came to realize was that it simply meant to leave your money problems, girlfriend woes, party stories, etc. behind and just come to work with a clear head and open mind. I can honestly say that I did that diligently every shift!

Sauces

STOCKS

THE MAKING OF STOCKS, dear reader, is one of the reasons I've been hesitant to write a book describing how we cook at S.N.O.B. This foundation of the French kitchen is what's set us apart from the beginning. It's fundamental to our rhythm of cuisine, and yet 99% of you won't make them at home—I don't!

At S.N.O.B., we make stocks out of most everything we have: veal, pork, chicken, duck, pigeon, lamb, fish, shrimp, and so on. Some we blanch and cook blond, some we roast and cook brown, or add browned meat scraps as rhythm dictates—it all adds up to a lot of hard, dangerous work that is nonstop all day, every day.

The result is a rhythm of beautiful, flavorful stocks that I liken to an artists' palette. We skim, strain, and chill our stocks only to de-fat them. Then we cook, skim, reduce, and strain again, intensifying and purifying as we go, until we have the essence of the flavor we need. That's the beginning of our palette, the primary colors that we draw from to blend and weave and create juxtapositions of flavors, colors, and textures that meld pleasingly in the eye, nose, mouth, stomach, and intestines.

When the stock pushes the scum and impurities to the semi-circular side of the pot then its smiling and the stock is set

Stock Method

For a blond stock, such as **Chicken** (*p. 150*), don't roast bones or add tomato paste.

For brown stock—such as beef, veal, or poultry—roast bones until crispy brown.

Discard liquid fat, deglaze the pan, and toss into a stock pot.

Fill pot with water and boil, skimming the fat, then reduce to a gentle simmer (a smile) and add *mirepoix* (a raft), a small amount of tomato paste, and a bouquet garni.

Simmer gently and skim for hours.

Strain off this first run (saving the bones for a second run in a braising jus) and reduce by ½, skimming continuously, then chill overnight.

Next day, remove fat and reduce remaining stock again by ½, skimming continuously until you reach a shiny jelly of tight, clean reduced stock, ready for sauce preparation.

Chicken Stock

Chicken should be a blond stock, made without tomato paste, brought to a boil, and then brought to a smile, all the while skimming aggressively to remove the coagulated blood and fat. You're looking for crystal clear, clean, bright flavors. The whole process should take 2–3 hours.

Fish Stock

We like to make a rich, gelatinous stock from fish bones and pair the reduced stock with the type of fish it came from.

Tools needed: large pot, fine *chinoise*

Yield: depends on size/ quantity of fish

Ingredients:

fresh grouper skeleton

grouper head with gills removed

1 cup *mirepoix*

1 bouquet garni

- o 2 bay leaves
- o 1 whole garlic, peeled
- o 2 fennel fronds
- o 1 sprig fresh parsley
- o 1 sprig fresh thyme

Method:

- Rinse bones to clean off any residual blood.
- Place bones and head in pot and cover just barely with cold water.
- Bring to a boil, skimming any foam and scum that rises to the top.
- Turn down heat to a gentle simmer and add mirepoix and bouquet garni.
- Let simmer 1½–2 hours, skimming as needed.
- Strain.

Shrimp Stock

If you can get local shrimp with the heads on, use them! The heads are where the most flavor is.

Tools needed: 2-gallon pot, fine *chinoise*

Yield: 4 cups

Ingredients:

½ cup olive oil

4 cups shrimp shells (~2 pounds shrimp)

1 cup onion, medium-diced

1 cup carrot, medium-diced

½ cup celery, medium-diced

1 cup fresh tomato, medium-diced

1 teaspoon fennel seed

2 tablespoons garlic

4½ cups water

Method:

- Toast the shrimp shells in olive oil in the pot until pink and fragrant.
- Add the onion, carrot, celery, and fennel seed and cook without burning until the vegetables relax, giving up some of their rigidity.
- Add the tomato and garlic and cook 5 minutes.
- Add the water, bring to a boil, skim, and simmer for 30 minutes. Strain through a fine *chinoise*.

Neck Bone, Ham Hock, Pig Tail Stock

Tools needed: 2-gallon pot

Yield: 6–8 cups stock and 1 pound meat

Ingredients:

1 pound pork neck bone, smoked

1 pound pig tail, smoked

1 pound ham hock, smoked

1 gallon water

Method:

- Place all smoked pig sections in pot with water.
- Bring to a boil, skim, turn heat to low, cover, and cook for 3 hours.
- Strain stock through a *chinoise* and reserve meat.
- Refrigerate strained stock overnight.
- While still warm, pick meat and skin from bones, chop, and refrigerate separately.
- The next day, remove fat and use stock as needed.

Meghan Lee

I began working at S.N.O.B. at age fourteen. My favorite part of the day was standing next to my father in the kitchen, catching up on our lives as he prepared for the busy night ahead. It was through him that I came to understand the restaurant as a conduit of energy—energy of the earth through farmers and chefs, energy between coworkers, and energy between staff and guests. I was so proud of the mission of S.N.O.B. that every phone conversation, every smile, was meaningful to me. Loyal patrons became dear friends. Creating community is a real and beautiful thing. It expands home. I have my father to thank for making my home bigger and bigger, for teaching me how to keep turning the wheel.

REDUCTIONS

WHEN I STARTED WORKING for my great mentor, Malcolm Hudson, he blew my mind with his reduction sauces. Early on he said to me, "Here, taste this sauce that goes with the lamb."

"Okay," I said. "Man, that's really good!"

"It took three days to make," he said.

"Get out of here," I said. "Three days? No way. You're jiving me."

Even though I was no stranger to food when I started working with Hudson, I'd never heard of a reduction sauce, and apparently not many other people in the States had, either. They take an awful lot of time, effort, and love to make. They're part of the rhythm, part of using things up.

Reduction Method

Once you've prepared a sauce-ready **Stock** (*P. 170*), sweat shallots or onions and vegetables in a little butter, reduce with an acid (wine, liquor, vinegar) to slush, then add reduced stock, herbs, and spices, and simmer gently until desired flavor and viscosity is achieved.

Pass the final sauce through a *chinoise*, unless you want to leave the vegetables or spices in.

All the following reductions make 3 cups ——

Port Wine Reduction Sauce

Ingredients:

- 2 cups shallots, sliced
- 1 tablespoon butter
- ½ teaspoon salt
- ½ cup prunes, medium-diced
- 2 cups port wine
- ½ cup balsamic vinegar
- 1 quart reduced brown **Stock** (*p. 170*)
- ¼ teaspoon ground pepper

Follow reduction method to prepare.

NOTE: Add prunes and pepper at same time as stock. Strain. For service, enrich with ruby port.

Sherry Reduction Sauce

Ingredients:

- 1 cup shallots, sliced
- 1 tablespoon butter
- ½ teaspoon salt
- 2 cups sherry wine vinegar
- 1 quart reduced brown **Stock** (*p. 170*)

Follow reduction method to prepare.

NOTE: Do not strain. Leave shallots in sauce.

Honey Thyme Reduction

Ingredients:

- 1 cup medium shallots, julienned
- 2 tablespoons butter
- 1 teaspoon sugar
- 1 cup sherry vinegar
- 1 cup *verjus*
- 1 quart reduced brown **Stock** (*p. 170*)
- 2 tablespoons thyme, medium-diced
- 1 tablespoon lemon zest
- 2 tablespoons honey
- ¼ teaspoon salt
- ¼ teaspoon pepper

Follow reduction method to prepare.

NOTE: Add thyme, lemon zest, honey, salt, and pepper after stock added and reduction becomes shiny. Take off heat and let steep 20 minutes. Strain.

Green Peppercorn Reduction Sauce

Ingredients:

- 1 cup red onion, finely diced
- 1 tablespoon butter
- 1 teaspoon salt
- ½ cup brandy
- 1 quart reduced brown **Stock** (*p. 170*)
- 2 tablespoons green peppercorns, drained

Follow reduction method to prepare.

NOTE: Add peppercorns last. Do not strain.

Rosemary Red Wine Reduction Sauce

Ingredients:

- ½ cup carrots, medium-diced
- ½ cup yellow onion, medium-diced
- 2 tablespoons butter
- 2 cups red wine
- 1 quart reduced brown **Stock** (*p. 170*)
- 1 tablespoon dried rosemary
- ¼ teaspoon salt
- ¼ teaspoon pepper
- 2 tablespoons butter
- 2 tablespoons garlic, medium-diced

Follow reduction method to prepare

NOTE: Add rosemary and garlic at the end, take off heat and let steep 10 minutes. Add salt and pepper and strain.

Madeira Reduction Sauce

Ingredients:

- 1 cup shallots, diced
- 2 tablespoons butter
- ¼ teaspoon salt
- 2 cups Madeira
- 1 quart reduced brown **Stock** (*p. 170*)

Follow reduction method to prepare.

NOTE: Do not strain. Leave shallots in sauce.

VINAIGRETTES

I never met a vinegar I didn't like! — cf

Sherry Wine Vinegar Walnut Oil Dressing

This lends itself well to meat and poultry, such as hot confit duck or hot sweetbreads, tossed with a tart salad.

Tools needed: whisk

Yield: 1½ cups

Ingredients:

3 tablespoons shallots

⅓ cup sherry vinegar

1 cup walnut oil

½ tablespoon fresh thyme, medium-diced

½ tablespoon garlic, medium-diced

1 teaspoon salt

½ teaspoon pepper

Method:

· Whisk all ingredients together.

Red Wine Dijon Vinaigrette

An aggressive, tart vinaigrette.

Tools needed: whisk

Yield: 1 quart

Ingredients:

½ cup Dijon mustard

1 cup red wine vinegar

3 cups olive oil

2 teaspoons dry oregano

2 teaspoons dry basil

1 tablespoon sugar

1 tablespoon granulated garlic

1 teaspoon salt

1 teaspoon pepper

Method:

· Combine Dijon and vinegar.

· Add herbs, sugar, and garlic.

· Whisk into oil until emulsified.

· Season with salt and pepper.

Balsamic Vinaigrette

A milder, sweeter counterpart to the red wine Dijon vinaigrette.

Tools needed: whisk

Yield: 6 quarts

Ingredients:

½ cup Dijon mustard

1 cup balsamic vinegar

½ cup water

3 cups olive oil

1 tablespoon salt

1 tablespoon pepper

½ cup honey

Method:

· Combine Dijon, honey, water, and vinegar.

· Whisk in oil until emulsified.

· Season with salt and pepper.

Lemon Shallot Dressing

Add poppy seeds and serve with avocados, grapefruit supreme, and butter lettuce, or batons of poached parsnips and carrots—yum!

Yield: 3 cups

Ingredients:

1 cup lemon juice

½ cup shallots, minced

2 teaspoons salt

3 tablespoons sugar

1 teaspoon white pepper, ground

2 cups olive oil

1 teaspoon thyme buds

Method:

- Mix all ingredients together until salt and sugar have dissolved.

Honey Key Lime Dressing

A tart, sweet dressing.

Yield: 4 cups

Ingredients:

½ cup honey

1 cup Nellie & Joe's Key Lime Juice

2 cups olive oil

½ teaspoon salt

½ teaspoon pepper

Method:

- Whisk together vinegar and honey.
- Slowly whisk in oil until emulsified.
- Season with salt and pepper.

Tiny Vegetable Vinaigrette

This is a simple dressing that lasts maybe one day. The idea is to have a colorful vegetable vinaigrette with ingredients that reflect our *mise en place* at S.N.O.B. Yours might be different. That's okay. Just keep it light and bright.

Yield: ~4 cups

Ingredients:

⅓ cup sherry wine vinegar

¼ teaspoon white pepper, ground

½ teaspoon salt

2 tablespoons shallot, minced

½ cup fennel bulb, fine-diced

½ cup red bell pepper, fine-diced

½ cup yellow squash, outer yellow part, fine-diced

½ cup zucchini squash, outer green part, fine-diced

½ cup carrot, fine-diced

⅓ cup water

1 cup tomato, peeled, outer part, fine-diced

2 tablespoons mint

2 tablespoons parsley

½ cup olive oil

¼ cup kalamata olives, fine-diced (optional)

Method:

- Mix the vinegar, salt, and pepper together.
- Add the diced vegetables, water, olive oil, and herbs.

PICKLES & RELISHES

AT MOST SOUTHERN TABLES, like my parents' and my Granny Mobley's, you'll almost always have some kind of pickle or sweet relish. There was always something like that to accent a roast pork or roast chicken at our dinner table, and we make them on a daily basis at S.N.O.B.

Pickled Banana Peppers

We started doing these because, at the end of summer, the farmers always had a gazillion pounds of peppers that I didn't even know half the names for. We'd ask them what they had and they'd say, "Well, we've got peppers." So we got them and pickled them, and it worked out well. We use them in the salads for the salmon and put them in the veggie sandwich and in little sautés with vegetables or roasted salads. It always adds a zip.

Tools needed: 2-quart pot

Yield: 2 quarts

Ingredients:

4 cups banana peppers, sliced

3 garlic cloves, sliced

1 jalapeño pepper, quartered

⅓ cup salt

⅓ cup sugar

1½ cups water

2½ cups apple cider vinegar

⅛ teaspoon cayenne

Method:

Combine the water, salt, vinegar, cayenne, garlic, and jalapeño in the pot.

Bring to boil and pour over the peppers. Store in refrigerator for several weeks.

Variation

Substitute multicolored yum-yum peppers (lunch box peppers) for the banana peppers.

Robin's Dilly Beans

YIELD	TOOLS NEEDED
6 cups	large pot

SOME YEARS AGO WE did an event where we went all out making fancy *hors d'oeuvres* and for garnish, we used my wife, Robin's, dilly beans. At one point, the food columnist for *Parade Magazine*, Sheila Lukins, stopped by and tried a few things. I didn't think too much about it at the time, but about a month later I got a message from Sheila saying she liked my dilly beans and was wondering if she could put the recipe in *Parade*. I explained that they were in fact my wife's dilly beans, but I'd be happy to share it. When the article came out, she didn't mention me at all. Robin's Dilly Beans were in a national magazine. And Sheila was right—they're excellent.

Ingredients

2 pounds green beans, trimmed
2 cups cider vinegar
2 cups water
4 garlic cloves
½ teaspoon cayenne pepper
¼ cup salt
1 medium bunch of dill

Method*

It's essential that the green beans are of the finest quality and cooked tender.

Put all ingredients except green beans in a pot and bring to a boil. Pour over beans.

These keep several weeks in the refrigerator, but we always eat them before then.

Pickled Okra

YIELD	TOOLS NEEDED
4 pints	2-gallon pot

Ingredients

4 cloves garlic, sliced

3 dried or fresh
cayenne peppers

1 bunch fresh dill

2 quarts okra, trimmed

4 cups cider vinegar

4 cups water

2 tablespoons pickling salt

Method

Heat cider, water, and pickling
salt until boiling.

Pour over dill, okra, garlic, and chilies.

Cool and let sit until ready to serve

Pickled Garlic and Jalapeño

Tools needed: 2-quart
nonreactive pot

Yield: 1 cup

Ingredients:

1 large jalapeño, sliced

4 cloves garlic, peeled and sliced

½ cup cider vinegar

¼ cup water

½ teaspoon salt

½ teaspoon sugar

Method:

Bring to a boil for one minute.
Chill.

Sweet Pepper Relish

the secret weapon

YIELD	TOOLS NEEDED
7 cups	food processor, 2-gallon nonreactive pot

FOR THE LONGEST TIME, I thought this pepper relish recipe was my dad's invention. Then I looked in a lot of old Southern cookbooks, and they're almost all exactly like his except he added ginger and jalapeños to make it more exciting. We call it our "secret weapon" because it goes with about everything.

Ingredients

8 cups red bell pepper, medium-diced

4 cups yellow onion, medium-diced

½ cup jalapeño with seed, medium-diced

¼ cup fresh ginger, peeled and medium-diced

2 tablespoons garlic, medium-diced

3 cups sugar

3 cups apple cider vinegar

1 teaspoon salt

Method

Purée all the vegetables in a food processor—you should yield ~8 cups.

Combine all ingredients in pot and reduce until sticky, 30–40 minutes. Pay attention and don't let it scorch!

Feel free to make it spicier with more heat or a different color or type of pepper.

Pickles/Relishes

*Christopher Holme
with a couple days
worth of pickles*

Red Onion Jam

Tools needed: 2-gallon pot

Yield: 1 quart

Ingredients:

12 cups red onion, sliced

1 cup red wine vinegar

1 cup sugar

1 bay leaf

1 teaspoon salt

Method:

Combine all ingredients in pot.

Cook over medium heat, stirring occasionally, until sticky. Chill.

Marinated Cucumbers

A hybrid between Granny's icebox cucumber salad and Korean Oyi Namul, the role of this garnish for the **Old-School Grouper** (*p. 120*) is to give a cool, light, bright contrast to the hot, juicy, mustard-glazed fish. We enjoy the Korean version as a foil for spicy tuna rice rolls.

This salad is quick and easy, which is good because it's best eaten immediately while the cucumbers still have some crunch.

Tools needed: Japanese mandolin, bowl

Yield: 2 cups

Ingredients:

2 cups cucumbers, peeled, julienned, and seeds removed

¼ cup rice wine vinegar

2 tablespoons sugar

2 teaspoons fish sauce

Method:

Peel cucumbers, then slice lengthwise on mandolin set at 1/8" blade to make long, noodle-like strips.

In bowl, dissolve sugar with the vinegar and fish sauce. Add the cucumbers and serve.

Variation:

Add the following for the Korean version:

¼ cup green onions, thin-sliced

1½ tablespoons Korean red pepper flakes

2 tablespoons toasted sesame seeds

DESSERTS

At S.N.O.B., we make most everything in-house, and desserts are no different. But of everything we've served over the years, the dessert menu has changed the least. We'll run peach cobbler until we feel like we're going to commit hara-kiri by the end of summer, but then the seasons change and we'll switch it out to run something else.

Sour Cream Apple Pie

with Walnut Streusel

YIELD	TOOLS NEEDED
1 pie	springform pan, food processor

I GOT THIS RECIPE FROM Natalie Smolie back in the early 1980s when she and I were working with Malcolm Hudson at Weekapaug Inn in Rhode Island. I don't know where she got it from, but I was smart enough to steal the recipe and make it my own.

So few people make apple pie anymore, and many get discouraged with it because it's a dessert that's been taken to its lowest common denominator, degraded into a ubiquitous processed food.

This apple pie has been on the S.N.O.B. menu for twenty years, and every time I think about taking it off, I eat a piece and go, "Damn, that's good. Don't take it off."

It's simply a great *paté sucre* with sliced apples and a sour cream custard that you bake until it's set and then top with walnut streusel and serve with a cinnamon *anglaise*. It's a kickass, solid apple pie.

Ingredients

For Pie Crust (Paté Sucre):

3 cups flour, sifted

½ cup sugar

¼ teaspoon salt

½ pound butter, room temperature

2 egg yolks

2 tablespoons ice water

For Filling:

8 cups Granny Smith apples, peeled, cored, and thinly-sliced (5–6 apples)

16 oz. sour cream

1 cup sugar

½ cup flour

2 eggs, beaten

1 teaspoon vanilla

½ teaspoon salt

For Walnut Streusel Topping:

2 cups walnuts

¾ cup flour

½ cup brown sugar

½ cup sugar

1 teaspoon ground nutmeg

¼ teaspoon salt

½ cup butter, chilled and cut into medium pieces

2 teaspoons cinnamon

Method

Preheat oven to 375°.

For Crust:

In a mixer with paddle attachment, cream the butter, add the sugar, and beat for 1 minute, then add yolks and salt and beat 1 more minute. Add flour on low speed.

Briefly, before dough forms, add the ice water and mix gently until incorporated, ~15 seconds.

Place dough between two sheets of wax paper and flatten into a disk slightly larger than the springform and refrigerate 1 hour.

Roll dough out while still under wax paper and press into springform, pressing dough up the sides. Chill for 10 minutes.

For Filling:

Combine sour cream, sugar, eggs, flour, vanilla, and salt, and mix well.

Pour sour cream custard over apples, mixing thoroughly, then pour into crust.

Bake 50 minutes, until set.

While baking, mix streusel topping by pulsing all ingredients except butter in food processor. ~10 seconds, then pulse in butter until crumbly, ~5 seconds.

Put streusel in bowl and incorporate further with fingers.

Top the baked pie with streusel and bake another 20–25 minutes.

Allow pie to cool at least 2 hours before serving.

Crème Anglaise
(five-minute version)

Tools needed: 2-quart
pot, bowl of ice, whisk

Yield: 3½ cups

Ingredients:

8 egg yolks

1 cup sugar

2 cups milk

1 teaspoon vanilla

Method:

- Mix all ingredients in pot and cook
  over high heat, whisking continuously until it begins to boil.

- Keep whisking and place pot in a
  bowl of ice, continuing to whip until
  mixture is cool.

VARIATION

*For cinnamon anglaise: add 1
tablespoon cinnamon.*

Key Lime Pie
with Pecan Sandies Crust

YIELD

1 pie

TOOLS NEEDED

10" tart pan with
removable bottom, rolling pin

I<small>T WAS ONE OF</small> those hot days in the kitchen, and I was having trouble rolling out the paté brisee for a key lime pie. "There has to be a better way," I thought, and it struck me that my Aunt Helen, who was a talented cook and baker, had a great recipe for pecan sandies. It was practically indestructible, and we could easily roll it out between parchment paper and turn it into a tart shell, smooshing it up the sides and prebaking it. So we did, and that became the base for our key lime pie.

We serve our pie with a **Passion Fruit Coulis** (*p. 169*), which, before you sweeten it, is very limey with a super tart pinch to it. That key lime flavor, which is tropical, was stretched even further with the passion fruit.

Method

Preheat oven to 350°.

Lightly butter tart pan.

Cream margarine and powdered sugar, then add flour and salt in half batches.

Add vanilla, ice water, and pecans.

Form dough into a disc and chill 15 minutes.

Roll out between two sheets of parchment paper.

Lay crust in tart pan, smooshing the dough evenly up the fluted edges.

Bake on sheet pan ~20 minutes until light brown.

For the filling: combine the sweetened condensed milk, zest, and egg yolks.

As tart shell comes out of the oven, stir in the lime juice, pour into tart shell, and continue to bake for 10 more minutes.

Ingredients

For Pecan Sandies Dough:

6 oz. margarine (Yeah, I know, but that's what Aunt Helen used so that's what I use. Who said dessert has to be politically correct?)

6 tablespoons powdered sugar

2 cups flour

1 teaspoon vanilla

¼ teaspoon salt

1 tablespoon ice water

1 cup pecans, finely ground

For Key Lime Filling:

3 cups sweetened condensed milk

3 limes, zested and juiced (~2 tablespoons zest and ⅓ cup juice)

⅔ cup Nellie & Joe's Key Lime Juice

6 egg yolks

Kurt Weinberger
King Bean Coffee Roasters

Frank Lee and S.N.O.B. supported the local foods movement way before it was popular to do so. Starting out as a young man in business, S.N.O.B. was one of my first accounts in Charleston. They took a chance, staying true to their creed and welcomed King Bean Coffee Roasters into their restaurant. Working with S.N.O.B. was a big deal for my reputation and helped establish my coffee business. We've kept good on our promise to take care them, and they've been a customer of ours for over fifteen years. Frank Lee believed in us from the beginning, and we're grateful for that.

Classic Crème Brûlée

YIELD

8 servings

TOOLS NEEDED

propane torch,
8, 6 oz. ramekins, whisk

THIS RECIPE COMES STRAIGHT from one of my French chefs, José de Anacleto. To finish, we'd torch the sugar with a propane torch. People in the restaurant were freaking out about that, asking what we were doing to their food with a plumber's torch.

We've tried to take it off the menu, but people love it. It's one of those desserts that was popular a hundred years ago and it will be popular another hundred years in the future.

Ingredients

3 cups cream
1 cup whole milk
10 egg yolks
1 egg, whole
4 oz. turbinado sugar (or equal parts brown and white sugar)
1 teaspoon vanilla

Method

Heat oven to 275°.

Combine eggs and sugar and mix until smooth.

Add milk and mix with whisk.

Add cream and whisk to combine.

Add vanilla.

Bake in warm bath for ~1 hour, until set.

Dust custards with sugar and burn with torch until sugar caramelizes.

Triple Chocolate Devil Mousse Cake

YIELD

1 cake

TOOLS NEEDED

2-quart pot, whisk

To make this dessert we bake off the devil's food cake, cut little circles out of it, and sandwich it around a dense chocolate mousse in stainless steel molds, topping it with vanilla ice cream.

It's a terrific dessert, but we always have scraps of cake left over. So we mix those scraps with **Crème Brûlée** custard (*p. 191*), bake it, and serve it warm with ice cream and caramel to make a twice-baked chocolate cake. It is quite nice and another way we use things up, keeping it in the rhythm of our *mise en place*.

You're welcome to cut little circles and fancy up the presentation, but for cooking at home, this also makes a lovely 8" x 8" layered mousse cake.

Ingredients

8 egg yolks

1 cup powdered sugar

6 oz. dark chocolate (70%)

4 oz. butter

1 cup cream

Method

Bake devil's food cake and let cool.

In a stainless steel bowl, beat sugar and yolks over low heat until fluffy and doubled in volume. Let cool to room temperature.

Gently melt chocolate and butter together and temper into yolk mixture. Let cool to room temperature.

Whip cream to soft peaks, then temper ⅓ of cream into chocolate/yolk mixture. Fold in remaining cream.

Layer mousse on one cooled cake, then plop other cake on top.

Refrigerate overnight.

Top with **Rum Caramel** (*p. 201*) salty caramel variation.

Banana Crème Pie

YIELD

1 pie

TOOLS NEEDED

10¼" springform pan, 2-quart pot, food processor, whisk

THIS PIE HAS GONE through several different incarnations over the years. It used to be made with white chocolate with whole bananas chopped up in it, but it was a laborious process and easy to mess up. Then one of my sous-chefs said, "Why don't we make a banana curd?" And we said, "Yeah, why don't we?"

So we did. People love it, and even though we've tried to take it off the menu several times, they've demanded that we bring it back.

Ingredients

Graham Cracker Crust:

3 cups graham cracker crumbs

¾ cup melted butter

½ cup sugar

Banana Filling:

1½ cups bananas, puréed

12 oz. sugar

4 eggs

6 oz. butter, cut into medium cubes

½ cup banana liqueur

1 oz. granulated gelatin

2 tablespoons water

2 cups cream

Method

Prepare crust by mixing crumbs, butter, and sugar together. Butter springform and line with parchment paper. Press crust into pan.

Bloom gelatin in water and set aside.

Prepare banana filling by beating eggs and sugar together in pot, then adding banana purée and butter. Whisk over medium heat until thick and bubbly. Heat banana liqueur and melt in the gelatin. Add this to banana curd.

Remove curd from heat, place in bowl, and let cool to room temperature.

Whip cream to soft peaks.

Fold the whipped cream into the curd and pour over graham cracker crust.

Chill overnight.

Serve with the **Rum Caramel** (*P. 201*) and a brûléed banana slice.

Peach Cobbler

YIELD	TOOLS NEEDED
4-6 servings	8" x 8" baking dish

WE'VE RUN COBBLERS FOREVER and always had enormous success with them. We make them with a cookie dough that's baked fresh, while the baking powder is very active, so that it absorbs the moisture from the fruit when it's baking.

We have a blackberry cobbler seasoned with sugar and vodka, a blueberry one with lemon, a peach with tons of bourbon and brown sugar, and an apple cobbler with cinnamon and brandy—literally a cobbler for every season.

Each of these is topped with a different kind of ice cream or caramel, which makes for a very satisfying dessert. The only issue I ever ran into was with old-school Charlestonians who wanted me to peel the peaches, but I like to wash them and leave the skins on. It tastes good and I think it looks good that way, too.

Ingredients

For Filling:

4+ cups peaches, sliced

3 tablespoons brown sugar

½ teaspoon vanilla

½ cup bourbon

For Topping:

¼ pound butter

1 cup sugar

1 egg

½ cup sour cream

¼ tablespoon baking powder

1 cup flour

1 teaspoon cinnamon

Method

Butter baking dish.

Blend brown sugar, vanilla, and bourbon, then add peaches, and allow to macerate in baking dish for 1 hour.

Preheat oven to 350°.

For the topping: cream the butter and sugar. Add egg and fold in sour cream.

Sift all dry ingredients together in separate bowl, then fold into wet mixture.

Crumble topping over peach filling.

Bake 35 minutes or until bubbly and brown.

Black Bottom Pie

YIELD	TOOLS NEEDED
1 pie	10¼" springform pan, 2-quart pot, bowl with ice, whisk

WE LIKE TO LOOK for desserts that you'd find in an old-school Southern diner, and Black Bottom Pie is about as classic as you can get. We've done a lot of variations on this pie over the years, including a version that's now an all-chocolate pie, and the recipe is pretty straightforward. It's layers of white and dark chocolate look dramatic on the plate.

Ingredients

1 **Oreo Crumb Crust** (P. 197)

5 tablespoons rum

1½ oz. granulated gelatin

1 cup sugar

6 egg yolks

3 cups milk

1 tablespoon corn starch

2½ cups 70% dark chocolate chips

1 cup cream

3 tablespoons powdered sugar

Method

Prep springform with Oreo crumb crust per directions.

In a small bowl, bloom the gelatin in the rum and set aside.

Whisk the egg yolks, 1 cup sugar, and 1 tablespoon corn starch in the pot until well incorporated, then add the milk and bring to a boil, whisking constantly for 2 minutes or until thick.

Remove from heat and whisk in gelatin.

Put chocolate in a bowl and pour 3 cups of the hot cream over it. Set aside.

Place pot with remaining cream on the bowl of ice and whisk to cool down.

By now, the chocolate should have melted under the hot cream. Gently mix until consistent and pour the chocolate mix over the Oreo crust.

Whip the remaining cream to soft peaks, gently fold into the chilled cream, and pour carefully over the chocolate layer.

Chill 2–3 hours.

Serve with chocolate sauce.

Chocolate Peanut Butter Pie

YIELD	**TOOLS NEEDED**
1 pie	10¼" springform pan, 2-quart pot

Ingredients

1 Oreo Crumb Crust (p. 197)

1 cup butter, room temperature

1 cup brown sugar

3 cups graham cracker crumbs

12 oz. natural peanut butter

8 oz. 70% dark chocolate chips

10 egg yolks

2 cups cream

Method

Prepare the Oreo crumb crust per directions.

For the Peanut Butter Layer:

- Cream the butter, peanut butter, and sugar together, then mix in the graham cracker crumbs and smooth over Oreo crust.

For the Chocolate Layer:

- Put chocolate in a medium bowl and set aside.

- Scald the cream and temper into the yolks in a separate bowl.

- Pour the egg/cream mixture back into the pot and heat until it thickens, whipping constantly.

- Pour over chocolate and let sit for 5 minutes, then gently mix the chocolate and egg/cream together and pour over the peanut butter layer.

Chill overnight.

We serve with a drizzle of dark honey and salty toasted peanuts.

Oreo Crumb Crust

Tools needed: 10¼" springform pan,
mixing bowl, food processor (optional)

Yield: 1 crust

Ingredients:

3 cups Oreo crumbs, ground fine

½ cup butter, melted

Method:

- Mix crumbs and butter until well combined, then press into bottom of pan.

Luna Pie

YIELD	TOOLS NEEDED
~6 servings	baking tray, 2-quart pot

WE CALLED THIS DESSERT the Maverick Moon Pie until it was featured in *Southern Living*. A few weeks after that issue went out, we got a cease and desist letter from a company in Tennessee, telling us they owned the trademark for Moon Pie. So we switched the name to "Luna Pie."

It is fun to make and it looks great going out. And people love it because they can smash it and eat it— the crunch mixes with the soft mousse, and that strong caramel makes for a great dessert.

Ingredients

1 batch **Rum Caramel** (*P. 201*)

For Mousse:

4 oz. sugar

1 oz. water

4 oz. egg whites

1 pound high-quality white chocolate

2 cups cream

For Pecan Cookies:

3 tablespoons butter
1 cup brown sugar
1 egg
1 tablespoon vanilla
1 cup pecans, ground
2+ tablespoons flour
⅓ teaspoon salt

Method for Mousse

Line a baking tray with plastic wrap.

Cut white chocolate into small pieces, place on plastic wrap, and put in a warm spot to passively melt.

Heat water and sugar over medium heat, allowing mixture to begin caramelizing.

Meanwhile, beat the egg whites by hand to soft peaks.

When sugar mixture is light brown and gives off a caramel smoke, pour the caramel slowly into the egg whites, beating vigorously with a whisk until incorporated, continuing to beat some of the heat out of the mix.

After beating the hot caramel and egg whites together, gather up the sides of the plastic wrap under the white chocolate and form a quick tube, squeezing the white chocolate into the meringue and beat until incorporated—about 2 minutes. Then let cool to room temperature.

Beat the cream to soft peaks and temper into meringue. Let chill overnight.

Most recipes call for taking the temperature of the syrup—undoubtedly a good idea. In forty years, I've never used one. Instead I was taught to look, smell, and taste.

Method for Pecan Cookies

These cookies are thin, crisp, and susceptible to humidity. They barely last a shift at S.N.O.B. before we have to make them again.

- Preheat oven to 350°.

- Beat the sugar, salt, and butter until smooth. Beat in the egg and vanilla, then the nuts and flour. Chill for 1 hour.

- Line a baking pan with parchment paper and scoop 1 oz. balls of cookie batter onto it, flattening each with the back of a spoon moistened in cold water.

- Bake for 7–10 minutes and let cool on paper.

We layer the cookies and the mousse, starting with a bit of mousse on the plate to keep it from sliding around, then drizzling the salty rum caramel over the top. This is an ephemeral dessert and can't wait a second to serve. The crunchiness and the smoothness, sweetness and saltiness, is sublime.

Soft Pecan Meringue
with Rum Caramel

YIELD

6 servings

TOOLS NEEDED

6 oz. ramekins, food processor, mixing bowl

WE'VE HAD A HARD time with meringues over the years because of the high humidity in Charleston. We tried dacquoise for a while, and vacherins, but there was no place to store them away from the humidity, and by the end of service those beautiful crunchy meringues would already be gooey. One recipe that Malcolm Hudson showed me, however, has worked well over the years. It's a soft pecan meringue done like a crème caramel.

Ingredients

1 batch Rum Caramel (*p. 201*)
½ cup brown sugar
1 cup pecans
7 egg whites
1+ teaspoon cornstarch

Method

Preheat oven to 375°.

Butter ramekins and add 2 oz. rum caramel to the bottom of each.

Pulse the pecans to a fine consistency in a food processor.

Add sugar and cornstarch, and pulse to fully incorporate.

Whip egg whites separately to a soft peak.

In a mixing bowl, temper ⅓ of the egg whites into the nut mixture, then quickly fold in the remaining egg whites.

Fill each ramekin with nut meringue.

Bake in hot water bath for 45 minutes to 1 hour.

Invert meringue onto a serving plate; the caramel will puddle down the side.

You can serve the meringue hot right out of the oven, if you choose. We prefer to serve it cold with seasonal fruit such as blackberries or peaches and a quenel of local goat cheese. The sour tanginess is a good foil for the caramel.

Rum Caramel

Tools needed: 2-quart pot

Yield: 3 cups

Variations →

Ingredients:

3 cups sugar

½ cup water

1½ cups water, boiling

1 cup rum

Method:

Cook sugar and ½ cup water until a medium brown caramel.

Add boiling water to caramel while still hot. Remove from heat and add 1 cup rum, being sure to add liquor away from flame.

Use bourbon instead of rum.

Strawberry syrup: ½ cup grenadine instead of rum.

Cherry syrup: add 2 cups dried cherries and ¼ cup grenadine

Creamy caramel: substitute hot cream for the 1½ cups water, omit the rum, and add 2 oz. butter.

Salty caramel: add 1 tablespoon salt to creamy caramel variation.

Be careful

Don't ADD COLD liquid to the hot CARAMEL —

It will explode and burn the crap out of you!

Chocolate Pot de Crème

YIELD	TOOLS NEEDED
6 servings	6, 6-oz. ramekins; 2-quart pot

THIS IS A CLASSIC that our chef, Russ Moore, improved. It has a crunchy chocolate topping with a touch of Bulls Bay sea salt. Lovely.

Ingredients

For Pot de Crème:

3 oz. dark chocolate (70%), medium-diced

4 cups cream

½ teaspoon salt

6 egg yolks

½ cup sugar

¼ cup coffee liqueur

For Chocolate Shell:

3 oz. dark chocolate (70%), medium-diced

2 tablespoons refined coconut oil

finishing salt

Method

Preheat oven to 300°.

Bring cream, sugar, and salt to a boil.

Put chocolate in a bowl and pour cream mixture over, stirring until smooth. Add liqueur.

Beat egg yolks in medium bowl, temper with chocolate cream, then mix yolks into chocolate cream.

Divide evenly between ramekins and bake in water bath for 40–45 minutes. Cool and refrigerate.

Next, combine chocolate and coconut oil for shell in bowl, place in double boiler and stir until melted.

Pour shell over chilled pot de crème. When hardened, finish with touch of finishing salt.

Gail and Denva Simpson

 This is my "Cheers," and I guess you could say I'm the "Norm." My wife, Gail, and I love to sit at the bar and meet people, and over the years, we've trained many bartenders. Our family knows if we're going to lunch, we're coming here—this is "The Spot." Three times a week for almost twenty years, S.N.O.B. has been like another home for us. In fact, there's only one time I remember almost skipping a lunch, and that was just because we were boycotting the removal of the deviled chocolate mousse cake from the regular dessert menu.

Sherry and Alan Sutherland

 If you are lucky once or twice in a lifetime, you meet someone who has a profound impact on your life. Frank Lee is one of those rare people who has impacted the lives of many. Frank's gifts and talents as a chef are legendary, but maybe the most important gift of all is his attitude of "catch and release": catching (parenting) youngins and then releasing them to go and be as great as he has trained them to be. Our son had the good fortune of developing his skills as a cook under Frank's tutelage at S.N.O.B. until Frank encouraged him to branch out and grow his skills in other kitchens.

Long hours and hard work are the norm at any restaurant, but few offer the learning that comes from working with a Southern culinary legend who, through his passion, dedication, and personality, inspires his chefs to grow and excel. Frank Lee's inspiration for cooking is shared in this book and through the work of the many chefs that have been blessed with his coaching, his wisdom, and his friendship.

The Beat Goes On

Slightly North of Broad is the result of Richard Elliott's entrepreneurial energy. Dick had the courage to move his restaurant enterprise from the unyielding Colony House—where he, general manager David Marconi, and I had toiled for two years—to East Bay Street. He was also savvy enough to bring along David and me as business partners to share in the fun.

In 1993, we closed the Colony House and opened Slightly North of Broad (a name Dick coined and one I was sure would be the kiss of death) two weeks later. I was wrong about Charlestonians taking offense to the name—but was so right to enter into the business marriage of Maverick Southern Kitchens. It became a fruitful relationship that lasted twenty-five years and beyond!

Dick describes us as a three-legged stool; remove a leg and the chair collapses. I've seen us as a triumvirate of complementary talents: David's tenacity in all aspects of service and operations, my ambition to build a brigade of chefs, and Dick's business acumen. (None of us wanted the others' jobs). Additionally, Dick's commitment to business with integrity dovetailed into my philosophy of regional cuisine with French technique. Together we shared the joy of operating Slightly North of Broad with hundreds of youngsters—a high percentage of whom have blossomed into successful food-and-beverage professionals—and innumerable guests with whom we hold cherished memories.

In 2015, Bill Hall, one of the most experienced service professionals in the country, showed his entrepreneurial spirit by purchasing Maverick Southern Kitchens. With his dynamic family, Mr. Hall owns and operates the high-energy Hall's Chophouse on King Street, whose loyal following is owed to Mr. Hall's expertise in providing unparalleled guest experience with the highest-quality food, beverage, and service. Bill's impact on the Charleston restaurant scene is big; his heart is bigger. He and I speak the same language. His generous support has made this book possible.

The beat goes on, the wheel turns. We dance to the rhythm of the *mise en place*.

Acknowledgments

Anything I've accomplished in this life has been the result of sharing, listening, and accepting help from others. I've always been impressed by how much better my ideas become when I gain input from family and team.

My wife, Robin, and my children, Meghan, Everett, and Jesse, have been a constant source of positive energy, recharging my soul batteries and girding my loins for restaurant combat. No way could I have made it alone.

David Marconi and Dick Elliott both channeled superior judgment into my growth, although neither shared my vision for a fountain and fireplace in the S.N.O.B. dining room.

Jovan told me to cook for the guests, not for myself, and that perspective has led to many cherished memories and friendships. I proudly acknowledge all our service team members who were my eyes and ears and kept me connected: Desmond Garrity, Patrick Saboe, John Kelly, Christina Coture, Frances Bramlette, Tracy Sirco, Chad Simpson, Bryan Austin, Tracy Fandrich, Julia Romano, James Wilson, Sarah Tucker, Kelly Hahn, Ashley Mulvay, Jason Beardon, Katie Hajjar, and Peter Pierce are but a few of the professionals that have made S.N.O.B. a delightful joint to serve our friends.

Much of my successful leadership has been the result of structured collaboration with my culinary team and I'd like to give a shout-out to some unmentioned influentials who gave heart and soul to S.N.O.B. In somewhat chronological order, they are: Nina Baffa, Jackie Jackson, Darren McNally, Patti Gagnon, Kemo, Essau Graham, Ken Immer, Libby Stritch, Joe Frazier, Jason Scholz, David Tetzloff, John Watson, Johnny Scof, Ramon Taimanglo, Joey Palma, Ryan Trim, Justin Hammerstrom, Chris Newsome, Chun Felix, Sam Goinsalvos, Shawn Kelly, Stew Lyons, Chris Stewart, John Melfi, Ricky King, Robert Berry, Hamilton Johnson, Josh Hopkins, Kristin Osborne, Anthony Gray, Chelsey Conrad, Braydon Sutherland, Megan Hutchinson, Chris Holme, and Miguel Vasquez.

So, too, in the same challenge of, "Here's an idea, let's see you improve it," much credit is due to editor Kristin Hackler, designer George Stevens, and photographer Bob Waggoner, who gave their unique interpretations to my vision of the book.

And to my friend, Bill Hall, who took a leap of faith, and to the chef community we have in Charleston, which has become an unstoppable positive culinary energy spreading across the planet.

I am in awe of the love fest.

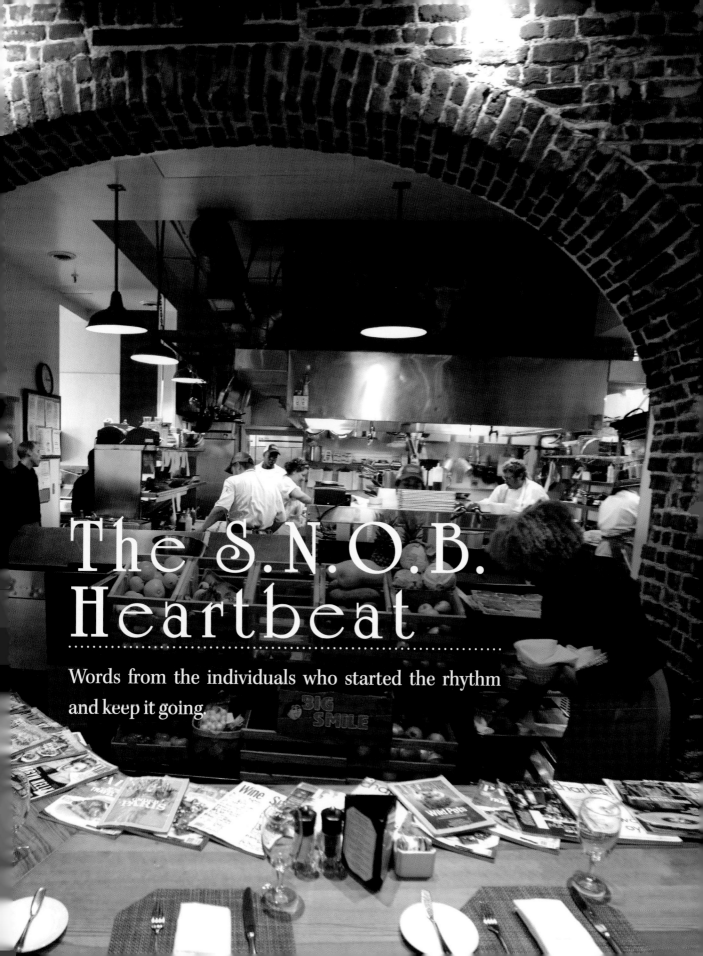

The S.N.O.B. Heartbeat

Words from the individuals who started the rhythm and keep it going.

Passing the Torch

Over the decades we have helped dozens of young cooks find their voice on their way to becoming responsible human beings.

Russ Moore, Chef of Slightly North of Broad, Cuisine Commando, has learned technique. He understands the rhythm of mis en place. *Now, in his own voice, he passes the torch, the spirit of cuisine, to the next generations. There is a whole lot of good cooking going on.*

Russ Moore

I came to Charleston to go to Johnson & Wales back when it had a campus on East Bay, and S.N.O.B. was supposed to be my externship site. I was going to be there six months . . . and that was fourteen years ago.

I already had a job lined up at Hank's, working as an expediter. I was going to be paid more, with tips on top of that. But then I did a stage at S.N.O.B..

The kitchen was unlike any I'd worked in before. Frank had surrounded himself with talent, and the way they all worked together was solid. It was like a tribe, every one of them completely dedicated to the restaurant, to the cuisine, and to him. It was something unique, a camaraderie you don't see in other restaurants, and Frank was right there in the middle of it, working the line.

At the end of the night he was still there, too, scrubbing the stove, squeegee-ing the floor, and washing everything down with the hot hose. He offered me a job by the dumpster at 1:00 a.m. while he was taking out the trash.

The pay was less, I'd have to work harder, but I took it because I loved that kitchen. There's the passion and focus of the crew, but there's also the actual physicality of it, with its open brick arch and seamless, mechanical blend between kitchen and dining room.

There's also this incredible energy to S.N.O.B.. On the days when the place is packed like a European bistro with a full line out the door, every chef squeezed in and everyone pushed beyond capacity, it creates this ball of energy—this hip, eclectic cacophony that's just loud and crazy and fun. Guests are packed in like sardines but they're loving it, too, talking and rubbing elbows as food swoops in from out of nowhere. The kitchen is too small to pull it off, but we pull it off anyway, and it's just incredible.

To cook with Chef is to know him as a person. His food is completely honest, with no pomp and circumstance to it, and Frank is the same way. He wears his heart on his sleeve, and whatever is on his mind, he'll tell you. His food is not about "keeping up with the Joneses"—it's about good food done well and with integrity, and hopefully the customers get that.

I'd worked in a lot of really diverse places before S.N.O.B. and enjoyed all of them, but I didn't find a home until I came here. It wasn't so much about the cuisine but about the culture and environment that Chef created, and I enjoy being a part of that.

David Marconi

If we could have bottled and replicated Slightly North of Broad, we would have. It's such a unique place, and it started with having good people. But part of it is the place itself.

The space is completely distinctive. You can stand at the front door and see the whole place. There's roughly a hundred seats and you can get as busy as can be, but you know it's controllable, manageable, and you can do all that at a high level. That's just another part of what I think makes S.N.O.B. as successful as it is today.

Frank and I started about a month apart from each other in 1991 at Dick Elliott's Colony House on Prioleau Street. He hired me as manager and Frank as chef. That place was eighteen thousand feet on three levels, and the kitchen was the size of all of S.N.O.B.. It was incredible, but after almost forty years it was getting kind of tired. Then Dick had an opportunity to sell it, and because the three of us wanted to stick together, he began looking for a place.

Somehow, Dick came across Nick LaPasta's, an Italian restaurant at 192 East Bay Street. It wasn't thriving—all brass and black lacquer with purple carpets, a drop ceiling, and sheet rock over that iconic brick arch—but he saw something in it, bought the business, and assumed the lease.

I can still see Dick up on a stepladder, punching through the drop ceiling and seeing just the apex of that arch. The first thing he did was to get the contractor to take down the sheetrock on the wall. Suddenly, the brick archway was there. It was almost like a miracle—we'd been talking about having an open space for the kitchen and there it was.

In designing the interior, Dick kept saying that he wanted a place that felt comfortable—a place someone could walk into wearing blue jeans or a tuxedo—and he worked closely with designer Janie Atkinson to make that happen. The whole place just has a wonderful feel, and people have responded to it well over the years.

Start to finish, the construction took about nine weeks. We closed the Colony House and two weeks later opened up S.N.O.B., running all the tables, chairs, equipment—everything we could carry from the Colony House up the street to the new place. A lot of great people came with us from that place and worked their fannies off to get us up and running on time.

When we opened, the food critic for the *Post and Courier* gave us a great review and not two months later, we were featured in *Southern Living* magazine. Slightly North of Broad has been remarkably consistent and relevant ever since, which is almost unheard of in the restaurant business.

The thing is, you could drop Frank anywhere on the planet and he would assimilate and be able to cook for anybody. He could hang with any of the top chefs in the world because he just has that mind. Whatever those experiences are that you gather over a lifetime, he's the real deal, the genuine article.

Dayna and Dick Elliott.

Dick Elliott

Career wise, I certainly did not start out with the goal of one day owning a restaurant. I was a USC journalism major who went to U of Michigan Law School. Then I was a trial lawyer in Atlanta followed by being an in-house attorney for a major textile company. My real business career started when the textile company selected me to run a division.

After several years of that, my wife and I returned to my birth town of Charleston in the spring of 1989 with the idea of buying a manufacturing business. At that time, however, there were few manufacturing businesses in the region. What we did buy was a great piece of real estate near the Charleston harbor that housed one of the city's oldest and largest restaurants: the Colony House on Prioleau St. The purchase was finalized just before Hurricane Hugo devastated the city.

The building wasn't damaged in the storm, but the tourism and business community were. We lost much of the core business base of the Colony House when they had to move out of town following the storm, so I ended up managing the restaurant just to keep it going. In 1991, David Marconi joined us as general manager, and in 1992, I was lucky enough to convince Frank Lee to join us as chef. We had a great team between the three of us. When the Club Corporation of America offered to buy the Colony House in 1993, we saw that as our opportunity to start a new restaurant that was smaller but also unique in Charleston.

Our goal with Slightly North of Broad was to create a restaurant that was at once inviting, comfortable, and affordable, with quality food made with care and integrity. We wanted it to be a neighborhood place—funky and fun and real—and we wanted it to be representative of Charleston in terms of cuisine as well as of the feel, the attitude, and the character. And that's what it became. I'm still struck by how many people tell me that this is the first place they take friends who are visiting Charleston and how many locals tell me how much this place represents the city. For years, one of the most popular auction items in town was "Lunch with Mayor Riley at S.N.O.B."

The three of us—Frank, David, and I—have changed a lot over the years, but we've stuck together through it all for more than twenty-five years. And each of us are still married to the same women! Frank, especially, has evolved a lot. He really was somewhat of a disruptive rebel when he started with us at the Colony House. At first he abided by his French training in the kitchen—ripping the hides off the kitchen staff; he was loud and profane. I admire people like Frank who evolve and grow, and he became a wonderful teacher and mentor as he continued to work incredibly hard and smart. Teaching has always been in his blood—his father Dr. Charles Lee was the SC archivist—and that mentality began to shine through. He takes so much pride in developing young people in the kitchen. He instills his legacy in them—his passion for doing things the right way—using everything and not wasting a thing.

It's gratifying to see how much Slightly North of Broad has evolved over the years and at the same time how it has remained such a constant in our lives and in the life of Charleston. I'm proud to have been a part of it.

Peter Pierce

I can remember the first time I ever stepped foot in the front door of Slightly North of Broad. I had been hired as a server at High Cotton, and after my shift, I asked if there was a good place nearby that I could go for dinner.

"Go to S.N.O.B.," they told me, pointing across the street. So I did. I sat down near the window—Carla was behind the bar—and when I asked what I should get, they said, "Try the barbecue tuna." I didn't know what to think about that, but I decided to give it a shot. Then I looked down the menu and asked, "What's a Big G lima bean?" They laughed and pointed back at the kitchen, "That's Big G back there!"

I got both, loved them, and I still have a hard time coming in to eat and not getting the barbecue tuna.

It was three years to the day that I started at High Cotton when I was transferred to hosting lunch at Slightly North of Broad. They needed someone there who would be a lunch regular, who would remember the patrons, what they liked, and would just take care of them. Since I came from a career background working in private country clubs, I thought that was right up my alley.

I had no idea how incredible a place it was that I was walking into.

The people here are amazing, not just the staff but the people we see every day and even the people we see only occasionally but that have become such a part of our family that it's a celebration when they come in. There are executives and families with children that I've watched grow up. There are retired couples and there are CEOs—there are interior designers, authors, professors, chefs, historians, and people from all over the world who've all found a home with us.

Every day, my favorite part of the job is still being able to stand by that host station, greeting everyone when they come in and saying good-bye when they leave. I love remembering their favorite places to sit, their favorite food and drink; I love the rhythm and the balance of lunch, and I love my crew! They make me look so good because every one of them is a professional and takes great pride in his or her job. Any one of us would do anything for each other and for our S.N.O.B. family, and we all know that.

I've been here since 2000, and I still love coming into work every day. These people, this crew, our farmers, delivery drivers, and everyone who makes what we do at Slightly North of Broad happen every day—we're all a part of this amazing family, and I wouldn't have it any other way.

Gerald "Big G" Henderson

I started working at S.N.O.B. in 1996, though I didn't exactly apply for the job. I was walking by the restaurant one day and overheard Chef Lee saying that someone hadn't shown up for work. I asked if they needed help, and he said, "Get to work!" I've been there ever since.

I've done a little of everything in that kitchen, starting with working the dish station. Then one day, not long after I started, Chef asked me if I could cook soup.

"Sure," I said. "What kind do you want?"

"I don't care," Chef told me, "just make it taste good."

So I made a pot of okra gumbo that I learned from my mom years ago, and he liked it enough that it's still on the menu today. The cornbread we give to each table is my mom's recipe, too, though I switched it up a little. The dried white limas dish I make comes from her, too, though I put a half stick of butter in mine.

From the very beginning, Chef, David [Marconi], Mr. and Mrs. E [Elliott], and everyone who helped build that business embraced me as family. And you need that; you have to be able to work well together to be successful at your job because in the end, it's a relationship. You have to commit to each other, respect each other, be there for each other through all the ups and downs and support each other no matter what. What we have at S.N.O.B., what we've always had, is something special. We have that respect, that relationship, that understanding, so that if Chef says for us to do something, it'll get done no matter what. We're family, and if it wasn't for them, I'd have been gone a long time ago.

INDEX

D

E

F

G

H

L

M

O

THE RHYTHM OF SUPPLIERS

Abundant Seafood
248 Magwood Ln.
Mt. Pleasant, SC 29464
(843) 478-5078

Ambrose Family Farms
2349 Black Pond Ln.
Wadmalaw Island, SC 29487
www.stonofarmmarket.com
(843) 559-0988

Anson Mills
1922 Gervais St.
Columbia, SC 29201
www.ansonmills.com
(803) 467-4122

Botany Bay Sea Salt
6959 Maybank Hwy.
Wadmalaw Island, SC 29487
@BotanyBayCarolinaSeaSalt
(843) 559-7233

Broken Arrow Ranch
3296 Junction Hwy.
Ingram, TX 78025
www.brokenarrowranch.com
(830) 367-5875

Bulls Bay Saltworks
PO Box 656
McClellanville, SC 29458
www.bullsbaysaltworks.com
(843) 887-3007

Carolina Plantation Rice
1515 Mont Clare Rd.
Darlington, SC 29540
www.carolinaplantationrice.com
(843) 395-0657

Cherry Point Seafood
2789 Cherry Point Rd.
Wadmalaw Island, SC 29487
(843) 559-0858

City Roots
1005 Airport Blvd.
Columbia, SC 29205
www.cityroots.org
(803) 254-2302

Clammer Dave's
9988 Hwy. 17
McClellanville, SC 29458
www.clammerdave.com
(843) 343-2970

Curated Selections
1014 Governors Rd.
Mt. Pleasant, SC 29464
(843) 830-1254

Crosby's Seafood
2223 Folly Rd.
Charleston, SC 29412
www.crosbysseafood.com
(843) 795-4049

Dean's Rabbits
268 Hill Top Dr.
Fountain Inn, SC 29644
(877) 892-6430
www.deansrabbits.com

Food for the Southern Soul
PO Box 30279
Charleston, SC 29417
www.foodforthesouthernsoul.com
(800) 538-0003

Geechie Boy Mill
2995 SC-174
Edisto Island, SC 29438
www.geechieboymill.com
(843) 209-5220

Green Grocer Farms
Maybank Hwy.
Wadmalaw Island, SC 29487
@greengrocersc

GrowFood Carolina
990 Morrison Dr.
Charleston, SC 29403
www.coastalconservationleague.org/projects/growfood

Heritage Farms
141 Arrington Bridge Rd.
Goldsboro, NC 27530
www.heritagecheshire.com
(919) 222-9496

Holy City Farms

Maybank Hwy.

Wadmalaw Island, SC 29487

www.holycityfarms.com

(843) 670–2516

Joseph Fields Farm

3129 River Rd.

Johns Island, SC 29455

www.josephfieldsfarm.wordpress.com

(843) 559–5349

Keegan-Filion Farm

1475 Keegan Dr.

Walterboro, SC 29488

www.keeganfilionfarm.com

(843) 538–2565

Kennerty Farms

1928 Rackity Hall Rd.

Wadmalaw Island, SC 29487

(843) 559–1179

Kurios Farms

354 Kurios Ln.

Monck's Corner, SC 29461

http://facebook.com/kuriosfarms

Limehouse Produce

4791 Trade St. # G

North Charleston, SC 29418

www.limehouseproduce.com

(843) 556–3400

Lowcountry Shellfish Co, Inc.

7195 Bryhawke Cir.

North Charleston, SC 29418

www.ipswichshellfish.com

(843) 767–9600

Manchester Farms

8126 Garners Ferry Rd.

Columbia, SC 29209

www.manchesterfarms.com

(803) 783–9024

Mepkin Abbey

1098 Mepkin Abbey Rd.

Monck's Corner, SC 29461

www.mepkinabbey.org

(843) 761–8509

Northern Seafood Express

219 Briar Creek Rd.

Greer, SC 29650

*www.facebook.com/
northernseafoodexpress/*

(864) 607–5246

Palmetto Pigeon Plant

333 Broad St.

Sumter, SC 29150

www.palmettopigeonplant.com

(803) 775–1204

Rosebank Farms

4362 Betsy Kerrison Pkwy.

Johns Island, SC 29455

www.rosebankfarms.com

(843) 768–0508

Split Creek Farm

3806 Centerville Rd.

Anderson, SC 29625

www.splitcreek.com

(864) 287–3921